Checklist for Life
for Women

Presented To:

_____

Presented By:

_____

Date:

_____

Checklist for Life
for Women

Checklist for Life
for Women

Publishers Since 1798

THOMAS NELSON PUBLISHERS®
Nashville

A Division of Thomas Nelson, Inc.
www.ThomasNelson.com

Published in Nashville, Tennessee, by Thomas Nelson, Inc.

Unless otherwise noted, Scripture quotations are from THE NEW KING JAMES VERSION. Copyright © 1979, 1980, 1982, Thomas Nelson, Inc., Publishers.

Scripture quotations noted CEV are from THE CONTEMPORARY ENGLISH VERSION. © 1991 by the American Bible Society. Used by permission.

Scripture quotations noted GOD'S WORD are from GOD'S WORD, a copyrighted work of God's Word to the Nations Bible Society. Quotations are used by permission. Copyright 1995 by God's Word to the Nations Bible Society. All rights reserved.

Scripture quotations noted KJV are from the KING JAMES VERSION.

Scripture quotations noted THE MESSAGE are from The Message by Eugene H. Peterson, copyright © 1993, 1994, 1995, 1996, 2000. Used by permission of NavPress Publishing Group. All rights reserved.

Scripture quotations noted NLT are from the Holy Bible, New Living Translation, copyright © 1996. Used by permission of Tyndale House Publishers, Inc., Wheaton, Illinois 60189. All rights reserved.

Scripture quotations noted NCV are from The Holy Bible, New Century Version, copyright © 1987, 1988, 1991 by Word Publishing, Nashville TN 37214. Used by permission.

Scripture quotations noted NIV are from the HOLY BIBLE: NEW INTERNATIONAL VERSION® copyright © 1973, 1978, 1984 by International Bible Society. Used by permission of Zondervan Publishing House. All rights reserved.

Scripture quotations noted NRSV are from the NEW REVISED STANDARD VERSION of the Bible, copyright © 1989 by the Division of Christian Education of the National Council of The Churches of Christ in the U.S.A. All rights reserved.

Managing Editor: Lila Empson
Manuscript written and prepared by Candi Paull
Design: Whisner Design Group

Checklist for life for women.
    p. cm.
ISBN 0-7852-6462-0
1. Christian women–Religious life. I. Thomas Nelson Publishers.
BV4527.C475 2002
248.8'43—dc21

                        2002005955

Printed in the United States of America

        03 04 05 06   CJK   9 8 7 6

Heart Attitude

I will listen for God's wisdom in every situation.

Table of Contents

Table of Contents Continued

Introduction

I will speak of excellent things, and from the opening of my lips will come right things. —*PROVERBS 8:6* NKJV

The Bible speaks about the value of wisdom. It encourages us to seek wisdom and find understanding. *Checklist for Life for Women* offers nuggets of wisdom and practical understanding to help you become the woman God created you to be.

If you are like most women, your calendar is full and your days are busy. Sometimes it's hard to set aside a quiet time to be with the Lord. When the day is filled with work, errands, homemaking, creative projects, participation in church and community events, and the demands of taking care of an equally busy family, it's easy to let your spiritual life get lost in the crowded hours. *Checklist for Life for Women* offers a simple way to find needed inspiration and encouragement.

A woman of God honors all of the aspects of her personality and potential. This book helps you think about ways to do that. You'll be encouraged to explore your creativity, to enjoy the small things of life, and to take time to listen to God's voice. You'll learn how the virtues of honesty, courage, and patience can help you cope with the challenges of life. Setting goals, working from the heart, and understanding your calling in Christ offer fresh perspective on how to express yourself in the world. Spiritual perspectives on meditation, prayer, and serenity give balance to practical ideas on beauty, children, finances, and community.

Each chapter offers scriptures, quotations, and practical lists that help you tune your actions and your attitudes into what God wants to accomplish in your life today. Simple ideas for everyday living bring spiritual lessons down to earth. Take an attitude test and see what you think. Choose a practical action and make a tangible difference in your world. Claim the promises of the Bible and discover God's provision for your life.

May you find blessing, inspiration, and practical help in this book to help you understand your faith and explore your identity in Christ. May God bless you as you discover new ways to fulfill your potential as a woman.

Every happening, great and small, is a parable whereby God speaks to us, and the art of life is to get the message.
—MALCOLM MUGGERIDGE

We see through a glass, darkly; but then, face to face: now I know in part; but then I shall know even as also I am known.

1 CORINTHIANS 13:12 KJV

On every level of life from housework to the heights of prayer, in all judgement and all efforts to get things done, hurry and impatience are the sure marks of an amateur.

EVELYN UNDERHILL

Beauty is God's handwriting. Welcome it in every fair face, every fair day, every fair flower.

—CHARLES KINGSLEY

Above all things have fervent love for one another, for "love will cover a multitude of sins."

1 PETER 4:8 NKJV

I shall not find Christ at the end of the journey unless he accompanies me along the way.

—ESTHER DE WAAL

Because of an emphasis on strong men, we sometimes overlook the mighty women in the Bible, but they are there: Priscilla, Phoebe, and Sarah. Or Miriam, Deborah, Huldah, Esther, and Abigail. These were not quiet retiring ladies who never let their thoughts be known. They did not wait to respond to action: they created the action.

BARBARA COOK

Let's keep a firm grip on the promises that keep us going. [God] always keeps his word.

HEBREWS 10:23 THE MESSAGE

Checklist for Life *for Women*

Always be in a state of expectancy and see that you leave room for God to come in as He likes.
—Oswald Chambers

We are His workmanship, created in Christ Jesus for good works, which God prepared beforehand that we should walk in them.
—Ephesians 2:10 NKJV

Trusting God

Divine Appointments

Do not boast about tomorrow, for you do not know what a day will bring forth.

—*Proverbs 27:1* NIV

No matter how you plan and prepare, each day brings its own unexpected encounters. No matter how predictable and mundane your life may feel, surprises always wait around the corner. These are called divine appointments. A divine appointment may be a wonderful contact with a long-lost friend or an unexpected emergency that takes you to a hospital waiting room. You may meet a new person or lose a loved one. You may reach a long-desired goal or may have to put aside a cherished dream. There will always be many detours, disasters, and unexpected delights scattered along your path.

Sometimes divine encounters can be dramatic and surprising. When the angel came to Mary she was afraid, but she said yes to God. Jesus confronted Paul on the road to Damascus, and Paul's entire life changed with that encounter. Philip met the Ethiopian eunuch on the road and ended up explaining the Scriptures to him and baptizing him. But not all divine appointments take place in unusual circumstances. God often brings people together in the course of their daily round. Paul met Lydia when he went down to the river to where a regular prayer meeting was being held. Peter and John were on their way to afternoon prayer in the temple in Jerusalem when they met and healed a man crippled from birth. A casual encounter can have life-changing effects when God is at work through His people.

Keep in mind that though you may be unable to change a situation, you still have control over how you will respond. When your plans are interrupted, take a deep breath and give yourself time to think before you react. Take care of the need that is confronting you at the moment. Look at each person who needs something from you as if he or she is sent from God. Say a quick prayer and ask God to guide you and give you patience and wisdom. Trust the process and be open to God's leading through the unexpected.

Realize that each encounter is a divine appointment, each problem another opportunity for God to show you His faithfulness. When a difficult situation arises, will you choose to rest in Him? When a desired outcome is delayed, are you willing to listen for the lesson in the detour? Are you willing to receive the unexpected gifts a day brings and be open to divine appointments?

I Will

Understand that I am finite and that God will take
care of the things that are beyond my control.   yes   no

Receive the unexpected gifts a day brings.   yes   no

Listen for God's wisdom in every situation.   yes   no

Look for the lesson in each detour, delay, and
unexpected delight.   yes   no

Be flexible when the unexpected enters my day.   yes   no

Remember that God works all things together for good
for those who love Him.   yes   no

Look at each person I encounter as someone God has
sent into my life.   yes   no

Things to Do

☐ Set aside five minutes to pray for God's guidance about a specific
situation that troubles you.

☐ Introduce yourself to a new person at church.

☐ Memorize a Bible verse to remind yourself that your life is in God's
hands (perhaps Psalm 46:1).

☐ Take a break in the middle of your busy day to rest, reflect, and regain
perspective.

☐ Look in the mirror and see yourself as someone God loves.

☐ Go to a crowded shopping mall, watch all the different people, and
think about how much God loves each person you see.

Things to Remember

The LORD performs wonders that cannot be fathomed, miracles that cannot be counted.

JOB 5:9 NIV

I saw that there is nothing better than that all should enjoy their work, for that is their lot; who can bring them to see what will be after them?

ECCLESIASTES 3:22 NRSV

God sees that justice is done, and he watches over everyone who is faithful to him.

PROVERBS 2:8 CEV

Why, you do not even know what will happen tomorrow. What is your life? You are a mist that appears for a little while and then vanishes. Instead, you ought to say, "If it is the Lord's will, we will live and do this or that."

JAMES 4:14–15 NIV

Trust in the LORD with all your heart, and lean not on your own understanding: In all your ways acknowledge Him, and He shall direct your paths.

PROVERBS 3:5–6 NKJV

Faith is not belief without proof, but trust without reservations.

—ELTON TRUEBLOOD

O Lord, thou knowest that which is best for us. Let this or that be done, as thou shalt please. Give what thou wilt, how much thou wilt, and when thou wilt.

—THOMAS À KEMPIS

Music—My Heart's Praise

A New Song

I will praise the Lord God with a song and a thankful heart.

—PSALM 69:30 CEV

God loves to hear His people sing. He created us to sing, and when we sing His praises we connect heaven and earth with a song. "Come into His courts with praise," the psalms say over and over. Music can be a wonderful expression of our faith and trust in the Lord.

Singing comes naturally to children. Think of the simplicity and innocence of children as they sing "Jesus loves me, this I know, for the Bible tells me so." Sometimes adults lose the ability to sing a song to the Lord. If comparison, rejection, and criticism have stilled your voice, let go of the old criticism and remember how it felt to sing to God with pure praise. God loves to hear you sing. God gave you the gift of music to worship Him and to express the eternal joy in your heart.

There is great power in the hymns and praise choruses sung in a church service. To stand in the congregation, joining your voice with others, offers praise to God that also speaks to your spirit. When you are alone, there is great sweetness in singing a little song to God. Do not worry whether you are off-key or what your voice sounds like. Give the gift of your small song to God, and He will be well pleased. Memorize a favorite hymn. Sing a worship chorus as you do the dishes. Go to church on Sunday and join in the singing. If you are shy about making music, read aloud a psalm of praise. Let your voice express your joy.

You don't have to be a singer or musician to make melody in your heart to the Lord. God is also serenading you. Hear the birds sing outside your window in the morning. Take time to listen to your favorite music. Attend a concert. Enjoy the music of nature, from a babbling brook to the wind in the trees. Notice the musicality of other voices, from quiet murmurs in a restaurant to jubilant cheers at a football game.

Music is to be enjoyed for its own sake, because it is beautiful and it hints at the inexpressible. It is also one of the ways God can heal, reaching past intellectual objections and speaking straight to the heart. God conducts the symphony of your life. You can sing a new song to the Lord with your voice. You can hear a new song in the sounds of your day. And you can feel a new song of gratitude grow in your heart.

I Will

Sing and make melody in my heart to God.   yes ___ no ___

Worship God with a childlike heart.   yes ___ no ___

Hear the music of life all around me.   yes ___ no ___

Renew my spirit through music.   yes ___ no ___

Create a new song and offer it as my personal
praise to God.   yes ___ no ___

Explore all kinds of music and share my enjoyment
with others.   yes ___ no ___

Remember that calming music can soothe me in times
of stress and that up-tempo music can energize me
when I'm tired.   yes ___ no ___

Things to Do

☐ Sing hymns and spiritual songs to God.

☐ Listen to one of the classics by Bach or Mozart.

☐ Join a volunteer choir.

☐ Listen to the music of creation: birds singing, wind blowing in the trees,
water falling, children laughing.

☐ Attend a local concert or musical performance.

☐ Give thanks for the way musicians glorify God with their creative gifts,
and pray for those who make music in your life.

☐ Worship the Lord with others this Sunday.

Things to Remember

Sing aloud to God our strength; make a joyful shout to the God of Jacob.

PSALM 81:1 NKJV

You will sing as on the night you celebrate a holy festival; your hearts will rejoice as when people go up with flutes to the mountain of the Lord, to the Rock of Israel.

ISAIAH 30:29 NIV

I will pray with the spirit, and I will also pray with the understanding. I will sing with the spirit, and I will also sing with the understanding.

1 CORINTHIANS 14:15 NKJV

Sing songs from your heart to Christ. Sing praises over everything, any excuse for a song to God the Father in the name of our Master, Jesus Christ.

EPHESIANS 5:19 THE MESSAGE

If you are having trouble, you should pray. And if you are feeling good, you should sing praises.

JAMES 5:13 CEV

Your statutes have been my songs wherever I make my home.

PSALM 119:54 NRSV

Nothing on earth is so well suited to make the sad merry, the merry sad, to give courage to the despairing, to make the proud humble, to lessen envy and hate, as music.

—MARTIN LUTHER

As blended voices fill the air

The soul could soar to worlds more fair,

Escape from prison bonds.

—MARGARET DRYBURGH

Forgiveness

The Gift that Keeps on Giving

As far as the east is from the west, so far hath he removed our transgressions from us.

—PSALM 103:12 KJV

Forgiveness is the act of pardoning another in spite of his or her errors, shortcomings, or wrong actions. God forgives sin. He is a God of grace and pardon who sent His own Son, Jesus Christ, to die for all humankind. Christ in His death and resurrection triumphed over sin. To be forgiven is to be identified with Christ in the full victory of His crucifixion and resurrection. His forgiveness is complete. Dwight L. Moody once said, "God has cast our confessed sins into the depths of the sea, and He's even put a 'No Fishing' sign over the spot." The Bible promises that if you confess your sins to God, He is faithful and just and will forgive your sins.

In the Lord's Prayer, you ask God to "forgive us our trespasses as we forgive those who trespass against us." Though you are commanded to forgive others as you have been forgiven by God, sometimes you may have trouble moving from intellectual assent into true forgiveness. A friend can let you down. You become a victim of crime. Someone you trusted betrays you. It is hard to forgive when you are hurt. But it is even more difficult to forgive those who hurt or mistreat your loved ones, especially your children. As a woman, you are fiercely protective of your family, and if someone has done something hurtful to those you love, you are more ready to seek revenge than to offer forgiveness. But your anger or bitterness does not resolve the problem. It only adds fuel to the fire.

When it is difficult to forgive, you must come to God asking for the ability to forgive. This kind of forgiveness becomes a healing gift. Forgiveness releases God to work in a situation and transform it. As long as forgiveness is resisted, you stay locked in the same situation—one adversary facing another, waiting for someone to acknowledge wrongdoing. Forgiveness is an act of pardon. When you pardon others and yourself, God is released to create a new dynamic of reconciliation and transformation—turning a negative situation into an opportunity for positive change. The gift of forgiveness can release you from the cycle of wrongdoing and blame.

Choosing to forgive is a tremendous step toward breaking the chain of pain and entering into freedom. It takes a great deal of courage to let go of the past, release the pain, and allow forgiveness to enter your heart. It means that you have to stop judging who is right and who is wrong. Instead, you learn to look past the behavior of those who hurt you and begin to see their pain and their need for forgiveness.

Every day there is a choice to make. When feelings of pain, sorrow, or anger arise, choose not to dwell in them and not to nurse old grudges. Acknowledge the pain, release it to God in forgiveness, and move on. When you are tempted to judge or criticize others, choose to replace your negative thoughts with a more loving attitude. When you fail to live up to your own standards, acknowledge your failing to God and then release your failure, knowing that as He forgives you, so you can forgive yourself. "Blessed are the merciful, for they shall receive mercy." The Beatitudes are a reminder that if you truly want to be like Christ, you must choose the path of forgiveness, just as He did.

You can choose God's way of forgiveness even in difficult situations. As long as you hold something against anyone, you hold it in your heart as well. And when you hold anger and judgment in your heart, you keep the door closed to God's healing power. When the situation is too difficult and complex to understand, forgiveness can release you from having to judge. And this allows God to work in the situation as He wills.

Give the responsibility over to God and concentrate on doing your part to make things right. Give the gift of forgiveness as an offering to God, trusting that He will work all things together for your good. C. H. Spurgeon said, "We are certain that there is forgiveness, because there is a gospel, and the very essence of the gospel lies in the proclamation of the pardon of sin." Open the door to love through forgiveness. Let love transcend trespasses. Let love transform your relationships. Forgive.

I Will

Forgive others when they hurt me or let me down.   *yes*   *no*

Be kind, gentle, and merciful.   *yes*   *no*

Give myself and others room to make mistakes.   *yes*   *no*

Remember that God tells me I am worthy of love.   *yes*   *no*

Choose to be like my Savior and forgive even in difficult situations.   *yes*   *no*

Know that God's forgiveness is a free gift, not something I earn.   *yes*   *no*

Remember that we are all struggling and we are all recipients of God's grace, mercy, and forgiveness.   *yes*   *no*

Things to Do

☐ Pray the Lord's Prayer, remembering especially the line, "Forgive us our trespasses, as we forgive those who trespass against us."

☐ Go to someone you have offended and ask forgiveness.

☐ Forgive someone you have been holding a grudge against.

☐ Pray a silent prayer for peace, love, and wholeness for our country.

☐ Send a thank-you note to someone who helped or forgave you.

☐ Let someone cut ahead of you in the line at the bank or grocery store.

☐ Make an appointment and talk to a counselor about how to deal with guilt, anger, and grief caused by the hurtful acts of others.

Things to Remember

Be kind to one another, tenderhearted, forgiving one another, just as God in Christ also forgave you.

EPHESIANS 4:31–32 NKJV

Be even-tempered, content with second place, quick to forgive an offense. Forgive as quickly and completely as the Master forgave you. And regardless of what else you put on, wear love. It's your basic, all-purpose garment. Never be without it.

COLOSSIANS 3:13–14 THE MESSAGE

> *He forgives all my sins.*
> —PSALM 103:3 NIV

Love isn't selfish or quick tempered. It doesn't keep a record of wrongs that others do.

1 CORINTHIANS 13:5 CEV

Who can discern his errors? Forgive my hidden faults.

PSALM 19:12 NIV

Blessed are the merciful, for they shall obtain mercy.

MATTHEW 5:7 NKJV

Let it be known to you, brethren, that through this Man is preached to you the forgiveness of sins; and by Him everyone who believes is justified from all things from which you could not be justified by the law of Moses.

Acts 13:38–39 NKJV

He has told you, O mortal, what is good; and what does the LORD require of you but to do justice, and to love kindness, and to walk humbly with your God?

MICAH 6:8 NRSV

According to His mercy He saved us, through the washing of regeneration and renewing of the Holy Spirit.

TITUS 3:5 NKJV

Through the LORD's mercies we are not consumed, because His compassions fail not. They are new every morning; great is Your faithfulness.

LAMENTATIONS 3:22–23 NKJV

Look through the eyes of your unfailing love, for you are merciful, O LORD.

PSALM 25:7 NLT

We need not perfect ourselves to earn the right to be loved. Love and mercy are not prizes for good behavior; they are the ingredients that allow us to heal and to become more fully human.

—WAYNE MULLER

Maybe the reason it seems hard for me to forgive others is that I do not fully believe that I am a forgiven person. If I could fully accept the truth that I am forgiven and do not have to live in guilt and shame, I would really be free.

—HENRI NOUWEN

Hospitality

Love in the Family Circle

May the Lord make you increase and abound in love to one another and to all, just as we do to you.

—*1 THESSALONIANS 3:12* NKJV

Hospitality is the gift of welcome, of caring for one another and caring for strangers. It is an open door, an open hand, an open heart. When we practice the art of hospitality, we reflect the heart of God, who welcomes all into His kingdom when they knock on His door and seek entrance. The Greek word translated as hospitality in the New Testament literally means "love of strangers."

Abraham hosted angels; he invited strangers into his house, washed their feet, and fed them. The Israelites were commanded to be kind to strangers. Psalm 23 includes a portrait of a host who prepares a table and shows every kindness. The early church was famous for hospitality and for sharing with those in need. And who could forget Martha and Mary, entertaining Jesus and his friends at their home in Bethany? Jesus continually crossed boundaries in the name of love, mingling with Jew and Gentile, rich and poor, important religious leaders, and people of low repute. In Isaiah and the book of Revelation, the scriptures tell about the supper of the Lamb, where all the nations will come to feast in the new Jerusalem that represents the kingdom of God fulfilled.

But the greatest image of hospitality lies in the image of the communion meal. When Jesus met with His disciples in the Upper Room the night before He was crucified, He broke bread and drank wine with His friends. He washed their feet and told them about the kingdom of God and His love for them. The church has celebrated this communion of bread and wine through the centuries as a picture of Christ's hospitality toward us and our hospitality for one another.

Hospitality begins in the heart, not in the size of the house, the lavishness of the table, or the elegance of the decor. We don't need a fancy feast, just our loving hearts and willing hands. We can show our love for God by caring for others. Whenever we entertain friends or strangers in our homes or reach outside our homes to care for others, we live out the love of Christ in tangible ways. The Rule of Saint Benedict says, "Let all guests that come be received like Christ, for he will say, 'I was a stranger and you took me in' (Matthew 25:35). Let suitable honor be shown to all, but especially to pilgrims."

An impressive home or expensive entertainment is not necessary if you wish to share the joy of giving and receiving. When you open the doors of your home, you open the doors of your heart as well. Some people grew up in homes where entertaining was easy. Shove the laundry over, grab an extra bowl, stretch the soup for one more person—voilà! Instant hospitality. But others were brought up to clean the house to sparkling perfection and concoct a lavish meal before guests were allowed in the door. Spotless, new, and expensive has nothing to do with compassion, connection, or fun. To make guests feel welcome, all you really need to do is simply care that they are there. The more comfortable you feel, the more relaxed your guests will be.

You can practice hospitality by reaching out. Welcome new neighbors with a first-night welcome basket with a new map of the city, the local paper, soap, toilet paper, instant coffee, rolls, and fruit for breakfast. Take a hot dish to a neighbor who is too busy or sick to cook. Treat neighborhood children to milk and fresh-baked cookies.

Hospitality is not limited to entertaining in your home or neighborhood. God's concern for the comfort and well-being of others extends to the wider world. Perhaps you can be a greeter at church on Sunday mornings or serve on a committee that plans congregational gatherings. Taking food, flowers, and comfort to shut-ins and those in hospitals is another way to share Christian hospitality. Visiting prisons, volunteering in community organizations, and offering your skills and talents to those in need are a reflection of Christ's concern for all of us. True hospitality is a picture of the heart of Christ, who welcomes us into the family circle of God's love for everyone.

Jesus said, "You shall love your neighbor as yourself."

—Matthew 22:39 NKJV

I Will

Be open to new ideas, tolerant of strangers, and
willing to extend hospitality to those who are different
from me.   _yes_   _no_

Look for the positive in people, appreciating differences
and enjoying the ways we are the same.   _yes_   _no_

Open my heart to new possibilities for reaching out to
others with hospitality and grace.   _yes_   _no_

Remember that I am loved by God and have unique
gifts to offer others.   _yes_   _no_

Care about the people who share my home as much as
I care for those who visit my home.   _yes_   _no_

Concentrate on helping others having a good time.   _yes_   _no_

Things to Do

☐ Invite a handful of friends over for dessert and coffee.

☐ Join the hospitality committee at church.

☐ Buy a cookbook or party book that will give you ideas for easy
entertaining.

☐ Invite a visiting missionary or Christian worker to join you for a family
dinner.

☐ Pamper a discouraged friend with a special tea celebration.

☐ Visit a shut-in at a hospital or nursing home.

☐ Bake a batch of cookies or a loaf of bread to share with the neighbors.

Things to Remember

Do not forget to entertain strangers, for by so doing some have unwittingly entertained angels.

HEBREWS 13:2 NKJV

Through wisdom a house is built, and by understanding it is established; by knowledge the rooms are filled with all precious and pleasant riches.

PROVERBS 24:3–4 NKJV

Share with God's people who are in need.
Practice hospitality.
—ROMANS 12:13 NIV

Be hospitable to one another without grumbling.

1 PETER 4:9 NKJV

Have we not all one Father? Did not one God create us? Why do we profane the covenant of our fathers by breaking faith with one another?

MALACHI 2:10 NIV

All the law is fulfilled in one word, even in this: "You shall love your neighbor as yourself."

GALATIANS 5:14 NKJV

Jesus said, "The King will answer and say to them, 'Assuredly, I say to you, inasmuch as you did it to the least of one of these My brethren, you did it to Me.'"

MATTHEW 25:40 NKJV

Since you have purified your souls in obeying the truth through the Spirit in sincere love of the brethren, love one another fervently with a pure heart.

1 PETER 1:22 NKJV

Do not forget to do good and to share, for with such sacrifices God is well pleased.

HEBREWS 13:16 NKJV

Behold, how good and how pleasant it is for brethren to dwell together in unity.

PSALM 133:1 NKJV

Jesus said, "I was hungry, and you gave me something to eat, I was thirsty, and you gave me something to drink. I was a stranger, and you took me into your home."

MATTHEW 25:35 GOD'S WORD

Hospitality binds the world together.

—JOAN CHITTISTER

I learned early on that setting a table is so much more than just laying down knives and forks. It is creating a setting for food and conversation, setting a mood and an aura that lingers long after what was served and who said what is forgotten.

—PERI WOLFMAN

Strength

Inner Power

~~~~~~

They go from strength to strength; each one appears before God in Zion.

—*PSALM 84:7* NKJV

What is a woman of strength? Many examples of strong women are found in the Bible: Deborah, Esther, Phoebe, Sarah, and Mary, to name just a few. All these women had one thing in common. They had an inner strength that came from their relationship with God. They were strong without being obnoxious or domineering, free to use their gifts and talents to serve others in a living partnership with God.

The Bible shows that all God's people are strong—and that all God's people are weak. You are strong in His strength and weak when you try to do everything in your own strength. Real strength does not ignore your weakness as a human being. You shouldn't be surprised when you experience weakness. It is part of the human condition to face weakness. God accepts you as you are, a mixture of strong and weak. He doesn't expect you to be Wonder Woman. But you can tap into an unfailing source of strength greater than mortal mind or muscular conditioning. You can be a woman of strength in God.

The Bible has plenty to say about strength during times of weakness. You may have high ideals, but many times the spirit is willing while the flesh is weak. Yet it is in times of weakness that your greatest strength may be found—the gentle strength of God's Spirit working in you. The word Comforter used in the New Testament literally means "with strength." Jesus promised His followers that "The Strengthener" would be with them forever.

God does not need women who are doormats. Nor does He want women to be dominators. You do not have to feign helplessness and weakness. Nor do you need to intimidate or denigrate others. Margaret Thatcher said, "Being powerful is like being a lady. If you have to tell people you are, you aren't." You can have a quiet strength that comes from knowing who you are in God. It is a gentle power that grows from strength of character, wisdom, and purpose.

How can you be a woman of strength and power today? You can honor your body by taking care of it so that you can maintain physical strength and fitness. You can honor your heart by standing for your beliefs and not giving up when times get tough. You can honor your relationship with God by using your gifts and abilities to make a better world for your family and community.

I Will

Understand that all true strength comes from God.	*yes*	*no*
Have the strength to be kind, compassionate, and faithful.	*yes*	*no*
Choose to live in God's strength by faith.	*yes*	*no*
Stand for what I believe even when I face resistance.	*yes*	*no*
Work with my natural strengths, offering my gifts and talents for the greater good of all.	*yes*	*no*
Remember that being a servant reflects the hidden strength of God's love.	*yes*	*no*
Understand that when I am weak, God can be strong for me.	*yes*	*no*

Things to Do

☐ Give some time to a charitable organization or ministry that helps those who cannot help themselves.

☐ Take a class or seminar to learn a new skill or enhance a strength or talent.

☐ Enhance your exercise routine with some form of strength training.

☐ Read a book about the lives of strong women—from women in the Bible to heroines of the faith to modern women who accomplish great things.

☐ Make a list of your strengths and weaknesses.

☐ Examine your beliefs about femininity and strength and write about it in your journal.

Things to Remember

She girds herself with strength, and strengthens her arms.

PROVERBS 31:17 NKJV

The LORD said, "Do not fear, for I am with you; do not be dismayed, for I am your God. I will strengthen you and help you; I will uphold you with my righteous right hand."

ISAIAH 41:10 NIV

Be strong in the Lord and in the power of His might.

EPHESIANS 6:10 NKJV

Less is more and more is less. One righteous will outclass fifty wicked, for the wicked are moral weaklings but the righteous are God-strong.

PSALM 37:16–17 THE MESSAGE

I can do all things through Christ who strengthens me.

EPHESIANS 4:13 NKJV

As your days, so shall your strength be.

DEUTERONOMY 33:5 NKJV

Endurance develops strength of character in us.

ROMANS 5:4 NLT

Nothing is so strong as gentleness: nothing so gentle as real strength.

—SAINT FRANCIS DE SALES

Because of an emphasis on strong men, we sometimes overlook the mighty women in the Bible, but they are there: Priscilla, Phoebe, and Sarah. Or Miriam, Deborah, Huldah, Esther, and Abigail. These were not quiet retiring ladies who never let their thoughts be known. They did not wait to respond to action: they created the action.

—BARBARA COOK

Values

Choosing the Best

You will understand what is right and just and fair—every good path.

—PROVERBS 2:9 NIV

What do you value? What is most important to you? How do your outward choices reflect your inner values? It is said that reputation is what you do when everyone is looking; character is what you do when no one is watching. God calls you to integrity, to live out higher values in your daily life. The Bible helps you to discern what is good and what is just, helping you to align your values and priorities with God's will.

The early Christians lived with a vital sense of purpose. Their relationship with God motivated and directed every decision in their lives. They didn't make a list of priorities to sort out, but grew in their relationship with God and then expressed the values forged in that relationship by their everyday choices. Priorities may change from day to day or week to week. But values are the reason anyone chooses priorities in the first place.

You are constantly growing as a woman. As you mature in your life and faith, the things you value may change, reflecting your growth in Christ. You learn to value people more and things less. You become more tolerant of others and less judgmental. Achievement and outward success become less important than community and quality of life. Authenticity is essential, while impressing people seems less important than before. Honesty and integrity far surpass outdoing others and "getting ahead." You seek quality instead of quantity. You value your families and your friendships, knowing that caring for one another is a reflection of the eternal values of Christ. You take joy in your femininity without having to play into stereotypes and cliches. Honesty, integrity, and kindness become more important than power, manipulation, and coercion.

What do you value? Do you honor the Lord or serve yourself? Are you choosing to do good work in the world? Do you tell the truth—not only to others, but to yourself? Are you trustworthy and dependable? Are you loyal? What kind of friends do you cultivate? Where do you spend your money? Are you willing to wrestle with difficult questions or do you prefer easy answers? How do you spend your time?

Living out your values isn't about a "spiritually correct" list of dos and don'ts. It is about living life from the heart. If you are truly honest with yourself about what you value, you will naturally make choices that reflect what's important to you.

I Will

Listen for God's guidance and ask Him to help me
make the right choices.   yes _____   no _____

Be honest with myself instead of glossing over
unpalatable truths.   yes _____   no _____

Choose those things that reflect my highest values.   yes _____   no _____

Make wholehearted choices instead of settling for
halfway compromises.   yes _____   no _____

Realize that priorities change, but that my values are
the motivation for the choices I make.   yes _____   no _____

Cultivate loyalty in my friendships.   yes _____   no _____

Things to Do

☐ Take a look at your current priorities and see if they reflect your inner
values.

☐ Meditate on Psalm 15 to understand the character qualities that reflect
personal integrity.

☐ Eat a piece of fresh fruit instead of a sugary doughnut, and go for a
walk instead of being a couch potato in front of the TV.

☐ Balance your checkbook.

☐ Do a Bible study on character traits.

☐ Set a goal and do one small thing toward reaching that goal.

☐ Spend an afternoon with encouraging friends.

Things to Remember

LORD, who may abide in Your tabernacle? Who may dwell in Your holy hill? He who walks uprightly, and works righteousness, and speaks the truth in his heart.

PSALM 15:1–2 NKJV

Make sure you don't take things for granted and go slack in working for the common good; share what you have with others. God takes particular pleasure in acts of worship—a different kind of "sacrifice"—that take place in kitchen and workplace and on the street.

HEBREWS 13:16 THE MESSAGE

The humble He guides in justice, and the humble He teaches His way.

PSALM 25:9 NKJV

Show yourself in all respects a model of good works, and in your teaching show integrity.

TITUS 2:7 NRSV

David shepherded them with integrity of heart; with skillful hands he led them.

PSALM 78:72 NIV

Evil men do not seek justice, but those who seek the LORD understand all.

PROVERBS 28:5 NKJV

The serene silent beauty of a holy life is the most powerful influence in the world, next to the might of the Spirit of God.

—BLAISE PASCAL

I'd decided that I would make my life my argument. I would advocate the things I believed in terms of the life I lived and what I did.

—ALBERT SCHWEITZER

Guidance

The Voice of God

Your ears shall hear a word behind you, saying, "This is the way, walk in it," whenever you turn to the right hand or whenever you turn to the left.

—*ISAIAH 30:21* NKJV

How do you know what God wants you to do? How can you go about making decisions that honor the Lord? Though it would be nice for God to call with specific instructions for the next step you should take, He offers a combination of divine and human guidance instead. He promises to guide you, and to speak to your heart and your mind. How do you go about seeking His guidance in your life?

Start with the Scriptures. The Bible offers teaching, instruction, stories, and wisdom. Reading Scripture feeds your spirit and helps you make choices based on your allegiance to God's values and your relationship with Him. Spend some time studying and reading God's Word. Meditate on the Psalms. Though what you read may not apply directly to your situation, hiding His Word in your heart through study and memorization will attune you to the wisdom of God.

But general guidelines still won't tell you whether to

go to your state university instead of an out-of-town college, whether to marry this man now or wait, whether to leave your old job and go to work at the corporation down the street. Ask the Spirit to guide you. God whispers to your heart, if you will take the time to be still and listen. Set aside quiet times for prayer. Ask specifically for clear direction. Then do what seems to be the natural next step, trusting that the Spirit will show you one step at a time.

Circumstances offer another key to understanding what God would have you do. List the pros and cons of a situation to give you a better perspective on what decision you should make.

During times of stress and uncertainty, gathering with God's people is important. It is easy to get off track when you separate yourself from the body of Christ. Your church can be a wonderful resource as you seek God's guidance in your life. Many people can help you discern God's will, from someone in a prayer group or Sunday-school class to your pastor in a counseling session.

No matter how many ways you seek God's guidance, in the end it comes down to making a decision, trusting that His voice will speak to your heart. Listen to God's Word, the wisdom of friends, your own analysis, and your heart. Then step out on faith that the voice of God is whispering in your ear, *This is the way, walk in it.*

I Will

Seek God's wisdom on a daily basis. _____ *yes* _____ *no*

Trust that I will be guided because it is God's pleasure to lead me in His ways. _____ *yes* _____ *no*

Let go of my agendas and allow God to surprise me. _____ *yes* _____ *no*

Be attentive to God's leading through circumstances and the counsel of others. _____ *yes* _____ *no*

Be willing to wait until I feel ready to decide instead of allowing myself to be pressured into hasty decisions. _____ *yes* _____ *no*

Be open to new ideas and new ways of doing things. _____ *yes* _____ *no*

Step out in faith, knowing God will direct me one step at a time. _____ *yes* _____ *no*

Things to Do

☐ Write down all your options and weigh the pros and cons of each possible decision.

☐ Write about how you feel in your journal.

☐ Make an appointment to talk to a counselor or a pastor about decisions that are particularly troublesome.

☐ Go to bed early so you can be clear headed and rested instead of tired and woozy.

☐ Copy a promise from the Bible (such as James 1:5) on an index card and post it on the bathroom mirror as a morning reminder of God's faithfulness.

☐ Step back from the decision-making process and get fresh perspective by indulging in a time-out for play and relaxation.

Things to Remember

The LORD passed by, and a great and strong wind rent the mountains, and brake in pieces the rocks before the LORD: but the LORD was not in the wind; and after the wind an earthquake, but the LORD was not in the earthquake: and after the earthquake, a fire, but the LORD was not in the fire: and after the fire a still small voice.

1 KINGS 19:11–12 KJV

When He, the Spirit of truth, has come, He will guide you into all truth; for He will not speak on His own authority, but whatever He hears He will speak; and He will tell you things to come.

JOHN 16:13 NKJV

The steps of the godly are directed by the LORD. He delights in every detail of their lives.

PSALM 37:23 NLT

Don't try to figure out everything on your own. Listen for God's voice in everything you do, everywhere you go. He's the one who will keep you on track. Run to God! Run from evil!

PROVERBS 3:5–7 THE MESSAGE

We can make our plans, but the LORD determines our steps.

PROVERBS 16:9 NLT

I am satisfied that when the Almighty wants me to do or not to do any particular thing, he finds a way of letting me know.

—ABRAHAM LINCOLN

Hang this question up in your houses—"What would Jesus do?" and then think of another—"How would Jesus do it?" For what Jesus would do, and how he would do it, may always stand as the best guide to us.

—C. H. SPURGEON

Providence

Angels Watching Over Me

He shall give His angels charge over you, to keep you in all your ways.

—PSALM 91:11 NKJV

Providence is an old-fashioned word with a timeless meaning. Saint John of Damascus said, "Providence is the care God takes of all existing things." Providence refers to the divine care of God and to His perfect timing in your life.

God wants to help you and provide for you. But when difficulties come, you struggle to believe that providence is working in your life. A sick baby, a husband out of a job, a crisis in the family—your equilibrium is upset by crisis and you wrestle with questions of "Why me?" and "Why this?" and "Why now?"

These are the times when it's essential to step back, take a deep breath, and focus on God instead of on the problem. God promises to take care of you. Providence is God's provision for you and the outworking of His intentions for your ultimate good. You can choose to trust or choose to be paralyzed by fear. God's will is worked out in mysterious ways. When you choose faith over fear, trusting that God can make a way where there is no way, you can persevere through life's ups and downs.

How does this translate into everyday life? When you are not sure what decision to make, which path to take, or where to invest your life energies, ask for God's provision and then step out in faith. Trust that He can redeem even your mistakes. The Bible promises that God is in control and that all things work together for good, even in tragedies that seem senseless and terrible.

There are many stories of God's amazing care and divine influence in unexpected times and unexpected places. In *The Hiding Place*, Corrie ten Boom recounted the story of her miraculous deliverance from the Nazi death camps. Other people have told of encounters with angels that saved their lives or prevented them from harm. People have told stories of missing the flight that crashed or of receiving an unexpected gift of money just as a bill was due.

Keep in mind that God is your provider. When life seems overwhelming, know that God guides you one step at a time. His angels are watching over you, all day and all night. John Newton, a former slave trader and the author of the hymn "Amazing Grace," once wrote, "We serve a gracious Master who knows how to overrule even our mistakes to His glory and our own advantage." Know that providence is at work in your life in unseen, mysterious, and wonderful ways.

I Will

Trust in God as my provider. *yes* *no*

Believe that God's timing is perfect; that He is never
too early or too late, but always on time. *yes* *no*

Know that my prayers will be answered for my
highest good. *yes* *no*

Have a positive attitude toward life because I trust in
God's guidance and provision. *yes* *no*

Be aware that good that can come out of a bad
situation when God is in control. *yes* *no*

Make wise choices for my own health and well-being,
as well as for the health and well-being of others. *yes* *no*

Things to Do

☐ Do one positive thing each day to reach a cherished goal.

☐ Be an answer to someone else's prayer with a generous gift of help.

☐ Write in your journal about a difficult problem in your life that was
resolved in an unexpected way.

☐ Ask a group of friends to brainstorm alternatives and solutions when
you feel trapped by a problem or situation.

☐ Memorize a promise from the Bible (perhaps Hebrews 13:6) and say it
out loud when you are afraid.

☐ Go for a walk in nature and bring home an interesting rock or leaf to
remind you that God has many creative and beautiful ways to
accomplish His purposes in your life.

Things to Remember

Abraham called that place "The Lord will provide": as it is said to this day, "On the mount of the Lord it shall be provided."

GENESIS 22:14 NRSV

People may make plans in their minds, but only the LORD can make them come true.

PROVERBS 16:1 NCV

In Him we live and move and have our being, as also some of your own poets have said, "For we are also His offspring."

ACTS 17:28 NKJV

God be merciful to us and bless us, and cause His face to shine upon us, that Your way may be known on earth, Your salvation among all nations.

PSALM 67:1–2 NKJV

Are not two sparrows sold for a penny? Yet not one of them will fall to the ground apart from your Father. And even the hairs of your head are all counted. So do not be afraid; you are of more value than many sparrows.

MATTHEW 10:29–31 NRSV

By going a few minutes sooner or later, by stopping to speak with a friend on the corner, by meeting this man or that, or by turning down this street instead of the other, we may let slip some impending evil, by which the whole current of our lives would have been changed. There is no possible solution in the dark enigma but the one word, "Providence."

—HENRY WADSWORTH LONGFELLOW

Sometimes providences, like Hebrew letters, must be read backward.

—JOHN FLAVEL

Choices

Beyond Fear

God has not given us a spirit of fear, but of power and of love and a sound mind.

—2 TIMOTHY 1:7 NKJV

God gave us the gift of free will. We have the power to choose. We may not have a choice about what happens to us in certain situations, but we can choose how we respond. No matter what we face in life, God enables us to learn and grow from our choices. "Good and evil both increase at compound interest. That's why the little decisions you and I make every day are of such infinite importance," C. S. Lewis said. "Every time you make a choice you are turning the central part of you, the part that chooses, into something a little different than it was before."

For instance, you might feel trapped in your job. No matter how many excuses you may find to believe in your own powerlessness, you have more power than you give yourself credit for. You can choose to develop new skills, seek out different opportunities in the company, or search for a better job. Start by seeing what you can do to make your current job interesting and satisfying. Sometimes an attitude change is all it takes. If that doesn't work, perhaps you need to meet with a career counselor to sign up for a class to enhance your skills. You may feel like you're stuck in a dead-end job, but the truth is that if you don't do something to change that, then you are choosing to stay stuck.

Life can bring suffering, limitations, and restrictions, but no one has the ability to restrict or demean your spirit unless you agree to it. Remember the 1989 student uprising in Tiananmen Square? The world saw the haunting but powerful image of a single unarmed student standing up to a battalion of Chinese tanks—an unforgettable picture of free choice. The soldiers retreated from the square and didn't return till two weeks later. You may not be facing tanks and soldiers and guns, but you can make the same kind of free choice in whatever situation you confront. Victor Frankl, survivor of the Nazi death camps, wrote, "We who lived in concentration camps can remember the men who walked through the huts comforting others, giving away their last piece of bread. They may have been few in number, but they offer sufficient proof that everything can be taken away from a man but one thing: the last of the human freedoms—to choose one's attitude in any set of given circumstances, to choose one's own way."

Over and over God says to his people, "Do not fear." God gives us the courage to face our fears and empowers us to make right choices. Fear of rejection or of others' disapproval often causes us to compromise what we believe. Many times a woman will compromise her integrity in a misguided effort to placate or please others. Instead of molding yourself to fit models of femininity based on extremes of passiveness or aggressiveness, you can discover a more balanced and powerful image of what it means to be a woman of faith. Meditating on God's Word can help you make wise choices that lead to holy living. God promises that He will give you the strength and wisdom you need.

It is your choice whether or not you will stand up for your highest ideals, develop your God-given gifts, and create a satisfying and productive life.

Here are some questions to help you think about how you are exercising your power of choice in daily life: Do you speak your mind openly or keep silence for fear of offending others? Do you involve yourself with things that are important to you? Are you able to communicate your needs clearly? Do you feel satisfied with the choices you are making in your life? What do you need to stop doing? What do you need to do more of? What are you willing to do to make positive changes in your life?

The ability to make wise choices will help you stay faithful and become the woman God created you to be. You can focus on what is truly important, choosing behaviors and actions that align with God's highest will for you. You can make courageous choices that will result in positive change, healthy self-esteem, spiritual stamina, and a more fulfilling life.

Perfect love expels all fear.

—1 John 4:18 NLT

I Will

Make choices that honor my God.   _yes_   _no_

Have a positive attitude.   _yes_   _no_

Remember that when I have not chosen my situation,
I can still choose how I will respond.   _yes_   _no_

Be thankful for the choices I am able to make.   _yes_   _no_

Be open to God's guidance and unexpected help.   _yes_   _no_

Be respectful of others and honor their right to make
choices, even when I disagree with those choices.   _yes_   _no_

Be honest about what is truly important to me.   _yes_   _no_

Things to Do

☐ Get a daily planner and use it.

☐ Write out your goals for the week, the month, the year.

☐ Set a simple goal and follow through on it.

☐ Wait for twenty-four hours before making an important decision.

☐ Read an inspirational biography of someone you admire.

☐ Meet with your pastor or see a counselor.

☐ Write down what you accomplished today.

Things to Remember

Let us not love in word or in tongue, but in deed and truth.

1 JOHN 3:8 NKJV

He who earnestly seeks good finds favor, but trouble will come to him who seeks evil.

PROVERBS 11:27 NKJV

My choice is you, God, first and only. And now I find I'm your choice!

PSALM 16:5 THE MESSAGE

I have chosen the way of truth; I have set my heart on your laws.
—PSALM 119:30 NIV

We may boldly say: "The Lord is my helper; I will not fear. What can man do to me?"

HEBREWS 13:6 NKJV

The fear of man brings a snare, but whoever trusts in the LORD shall be safe.

PROVERBS 29:25 NKJV

Teach me Your way, O LORD, and lead me in a smooth path, because of my enemies.

PSALM 27:11 NKJV

Jesus said to them, "Why are you afraid? Have you no faith?"

MARK 4:40 NRSV

He hath shewed thee, O man, what is good; and what doth the LORD require of thee, but to do justly, and to love mercy, and to walk humbly with thy God?

MICAH 6:8 KJV

When you eat or drink or do anything else, always do it to honor God.

1 CORINTHIANS 10:31 CEV

Paul wrote: Stir up the gift of God which is in you through the laying on of my hands. For God has not given us a spirit of fear, but of power and of love and of a sound mind. . . . Hold fast the pattern of sound words which you here heard from me, in faith and love which are in Christ Jesus. That good thing which was committed to you, keep by the Holy Spirit who dwells in us.

2 TIMOTHY 1:6–7, 13–14

Jesus said to His disciples, "Stand up. Don't be afraid."

MATTHEW 17:7 NCV

One's philosophy is not best expressed in words; it is expressed in the choices one makes. In the long run, we shape our lives and we shape ourselves.

—ELEANOR ROOSEVELT

Every act is an act of self-sacrifice. When you choose anything, you reject everything else—just as when you marry one woman you give up all the others.

—G. K. CHESTERTON

Loneliness

Filling the Empty Heart

Let your conduct be without covetousness; be content with such things as you have. For He Himself has said, "I will never leave you nor forsake you."

—HEBREWS 13:5 NKJV

A woman's day is filled with many demands. Family, work, church, and community involvement can all be satisfying social outlets. But sometimes there is an empty space that others cannot fill, a time without the activities that distract and delight you. Your best friend is unavailable. Your husband and children are busy with their own projects. You may be experiencing a life change, such as an empty nest with the kids gone and little to do. Suddenly you're feeling pretty lonely.

You can, however, choose how you respond to feelings of loneliness. Loneliness comes when you feel separated from others—and separated from God. But you can be alone, in solitude, and not be lonely. Loneliness is the empty ache in the heart, while choosing solitude can make for a time of contented aloneness that does not need company to share its pursuits. You can turn the pain of loneliness into the quiet contentment of solitude, if you are willing to make some choices.

First of all, understand that you are not alone in your loneliness. It is part of the human condition—everyone has times of loneliness and sadness. God is with you in those lonely times when you feel like "a pelican of the wilderness," as the psalmist said. Know that the sorrow of loneliness is like a spiritual wilderness. And remember that God has met His people most intimately and tenderly in the wilderness. When your friends and loved ones are unavailable, you can still enjoy communion with God.

Second, do not allow the pain of loneliness to close your heart. When your heart is closed, others cannot enter. You unconsciously push people away when you withdraw too far from intimacy and closeness to lick your emotional injuries. Like a wounded animal, you attack those who want to help you. It is one thing to withdraw from others for a time of rest and personal refreshment. It is another to disconnect and stay disconnected. If you keep pushing others out of your life, you'll eventually find you've pushed God out of your life, too. Only you can choose to open your heart and reconnect again.

Remember that you don't have to stay lonely. You can choose to reach out in spite of your pain. Be quick to forgive when others hurt you or let you down. Take your loneliness to the God who comforts the lonely and sets the solitary in families. Let Him fill your empty heart with His love.

I Will

Be quiet and listen to God's whispers in the dark. *yes* *no*

Remember that God is with me in my solitude. *yes* *no*

Trust that this season of loneliness will pass in God's good time. *yes* *no*

Choose to have a positive attitude instead of a self-pitying one. *yes* *no*

Be willing to ask for help instead of proudly insisting on doing everything alone. *yes* *no*

Be compassionate to others who may be lonely too. *yes* *no*

Open my heart to share greater intimacy with God. *yes* *no*

Things to Do

☐ Invite someone over for dinner or tea, or make a meal to take to someone at his or her home.

☐ Put a picture in your wallet or purse to look at when you want to be reminded that you are loved.

☐ Listen to worship music.

☐ Call a friend or send a postcard to someone you haven't seen for a long time.

☐ Take a long walk in the sunshine, rain, wind—whatever the weather, go out and get some exercise in nature.

☐ Read a psalm or Scripture selection aloud.

☐ Volunteer at your church or at a local community organization.

Things to Remember

I will not leave you orphans; I will come
to you.

JOHN 14:18 NKJV

The LORD also will be a refuge for the
oppressed, a refuge in times of trouble.
And those who know Your name will
put their trust in You; for You, LORD,
have not forsaken those who seek You.

PSALM 9:9–10 NKJV

Be strong and of good courage, do not
fear nor be afraid of them; for the LORD
your God, He is the One who goes with
you. He will not leave you or forsake
you.

DEUTERONOMY 31:6 NKJV

Look right, look left—there's not a soul
who cares what happens! I'm up against
it, with no exit—bereft, left alone.

PSALM 142:4 THE MESSAGE

When the crowd dispersed, Jesus
climbed the mountain so he could be by
himself and pray. He stayed there alone,
late into the night.

MATTHEW 14:23 THE MESSAGE

*When you have
closed your doors and
darkened your room,
remember never to
say that you are
alone, for you are not
alone; God is within,
and your genius is
within.*

—EPICTETUS

*The soul hardly ever
realizes it, but
whether he is a
believer or not, his
loneliness is really a
homesickness for
God.*

—HUBERT VAN ZELLER

Style

Brains, Beauty, and Spiritual Balance

As a ring of gold in a swine's snout, so is a lovely woman who lacks discretion.

—PROVERBS 11:22 NKJV

Remember when you were a young teenager, wishing you could be beautiful and stylish? It was a gawky and awkward time as you sought to find your way through the maze of fashion magazines, peer pressure, and fantasies of Cinderella evenings where the ugly duckling turns into a beautiful swan. Eventually you realized that reality was not going to be as smooth and perfect as the pictures in a fashion magazine. Being beautiful meant more than just looking good on the outside.

There is absolutely nothing wrong with wanting to be drop-dead beautiful—or at least in making your outside package prettier. Perfume, a new dress, high heels, a fresh haircut—let's admit it, they're all fun and part of the femininity that God created for you to enjoy. But when it comes to real style, the heart and the mind, not the outward appearance, are what matter.

The greatest beauty secret has nothing to do with make-up or fashion. It is being a woman who delights in God. She is, as the psalmist said, like a tree that never withers because she has her roots firmly planted in God. Her vital relationship with God gives her the ability to look beyond the surface to the reality beneath. She looks for substance—a kind heart, a discerning mind, and a strong faith—instead of being distracted by outward appearance. She knows that all good things come from God, but that some things are better than others. The heart that seeks after God is the most beautiful thing in the world.

A woman of style and substance is gracious and kind to all she meets. She lives her life from the heart, not from the ego. She notices the people that others miss and never takes a service or kindness for granted. Instead of whining about her troubles or complaining about others, she looks for the best in people and situations. She's savvy enough to know that people can let her down, but compassionate enough to understand why they do. She has learned compassion and wisdom and is able to see God's goodness in others. She takes a balanced view of life—serious without being stuffy, warmhearted without being overly sentimental.

So go ahead. Try a new hair-do or splurge on a stylish dress. Have fun and look your best. But never forget that true style is a reflection of your relationship with God. Brains, beauty, and spiritual balance have it all over the latest trend and the hottest look.

I Will

Remember that while I can be distracted by
appearances, God sees the heart. _____ *yes* _____ *no*

Live life from the heart instead of trying to impress or
manipulate others. _____ *yes* _____ *no*

Cultivate my spirit by spending time alone with God. _____ *yes* _____ *no*

Appreciate beauty and creativity wherever I find them. _____ *yes* _____ *no*

Remember that kindness and compassion are great
beautifiers. _____ *yes* _____ *no*

Enjoy my femininity without taking myself too seriously. _____ *yes* _____ *no*

Be aware of others who may be struggling even if they
look like they have it all together. _____ *yes* _____ *no*

Things to Do

☐ Read the Bible story of Esther to learn about the power of a beautiful
woman who was willing to sacrifice her life to save her people.

☐ Speak a kind word the next time you are tempted to gossip
about someone.

☐ Take an exercise class.

☐ Cultivate your mind by reading a good book.

☐ Become an adult sponsor for youth activities so you can
mentor younger women.

☐ Go shopping for clothes that are flattering, comfortable,
and expressive of your style.

☐ Leave an extra tip for the hairdresser the next time you get your hair cut.

Things to Remember

Do not let your adornment be merely outward—arranging the hair, wearing gold, or putting on fine apparel—rather let it be the hidden person of the heart, with the incorruptible beauty of a gentle and quiet spirit, which is very precious in the sight of God.

1 PETER 3:3–4 NKJV

Charm can be deceiving, and beauty fades away, but a woman who honors the Lord deserves to be praised.

PROVERBS 31:30 CEV

Every wise woman builds her house, but the foolish pulls it down with her hands.

PROVERBS 14:1 NKJV

Though some tongues just love the taste of gossip, Christians have better use for language than that. Don't talk dirty or silly. That kind of talk doesn't fit our style. Thanksgiving is our dialect.

EPHESIANS 5:4 THE MESSAGE

Happy are those who do not follow the advice of the wicked, or take the path that sinners tread, or sit in the seat of scoffers; but their delight is in the law of the LORD, and on his law they meditate day and night.

PSALM 1:1–2 NRSV

Taking joy in life is a woman's best cosmetic.

—ROSALIND RUSSELL

Goodness in the heart works its way up into the face and prints it own beauty there.

—ANONYMOUS

Valuing Life

Open Your Eyes, Open Your Heart

Oh, that men would give thanks to the LORD for His goodness, and for His wonderful works to the children of men!

—PSALM 107:8 NKJV

There is so much beauty and wonder in the world around you. Beauty reminds you that God loves you, giving you a tiny taste of what one day eternity with Christ will be like. Yet you often forget to see and value the bounties God has spread before you. You get caught up in the concerns of daily life, aware only that the next work deadline looms in front of you, the children need new shoes, the car needs repair, and the bills are due at the end of the month.

There are so many wonders in this world. Are you awake? Are your eyes open? Is your heart receptive? "Beauty is all about us, but how many are blind to it!" exclaimed cellist Pablo Casals. God saw what he had made and saw that it was good. Do you take the time to see what God has created? Are you able to be receptive and totally present in the moment? All kinds of wonderful and amazing things are going on around you. An important part of the spiritual life is learning to pay attention. "Consider the lilies," Jesus said. Take a moment to stop and stare in awe and behold the works of the Lord.

Even when your lives are stressful and your problems seem overwhelming, you need to remember that pleasure lies in the heart. Your attitude affects your perception. Luci Swindoll said, "To experience happiness we must train ourselves to live in this moment, not running ahead in anticipation some future date nor lagging behind in the paralysis of the past. With wholeness and sensitivity we must live in the here and now."

The mundane things of life—a sack of groceries, a phone call, a carpool, a meeting—can be reminders of God's generous blessings. That van full of children you are ferrying to the soccer game is full of bright faces and eager young hearts. A friend on the other end of a phone reminds you that you are rich in support and loyalty. A crowded grocery aisle can be seen as a place of plenty and choice. These small wonders can make you smile with joy, if you open your eyes to the value of life in the here and now. Look into your heart and see that you, too, are a wonder created and loved by God.

Today is a good day to value life, just as it presents itself to you. Open your eyes. Open your heart. Receive God's priceless gift of life.

I Will

Pay attention to my life.   *yes*   *no*

Be receptive and totally present in the moment.   *yes*   *no*

See God in the details.   *yes*   *no*

Be curious about life and all its mysteries.   *yes*   *no*

Open my heart to God's grace as revealed
in His creation.   *yes*   *no*

Be aware of small moments of grace and little
epiphanies around me.   *yes*   *no*

Be aware of what is going on within me.   *yes*   *no*

Things to Do

☐ Mark out some time in your daily calendar for "life-appreciation breaks."

☐ Go for a long walk in a park or forest.

☐ Buy a single rose to remind you of the beauty of God's creation.

☐ Read Psalm 148.

☐ Read a book on natural history.

☐ Spend time apart with a loved one, savoring with an appreciative heart who and what he or she is.

☐ Treat yourself to a new flavor of ice cream or try an ethnic cuisine that you haven't enjoyed before.

Things to Remember

God saw everything that He had made, and indeed it was very good.

GENESIS 1:31 NKJV

I will praise You, for I am fearfully and wonderfully made; marvelous are Your works, and that my soul knows very well.

PSALM 139:14 NKJV

Consider the lilies, how they grow: they neither toil nor spin; and yet I say to you, even Solomon in all his glory was not arrayed like one of these.

LUKE 12:27 NKJV

Jesus said, "First things first. Your business is life, not death. Follow me. Pursue life."

MATTHEW 8:22 THE MESSAGE

The song was raised, with trumpets and cymbals and other musical instruments, in praise to the Lord. 'For he is good, for his steadfast love endures forever.'

2 CHRONICLES 5:13 NRSV

Happy is the man who is always reverent, but he who hardens his heart will fall into calamity.

PROVERBS 28:14 NKJV

To believe in God means to take sides with life and to end our alliance with death. It means to stop killing and wanting to kill, and to do battle with apathy which is so akin to killing.

—DOROTHEE SOELLE

At the back of our brains, so to speak, there is a forgotten blaze or burst of astonishment at our own existence. The object of the artistic and the spiritual life is to dig for this submerged sunrise of wonder.

—G. K. CHESTERTON

Finances

More than Enough

God is able to make all grace abound toward you, that you, always having all sufficiency in all things, may have an abundance for every good work.

—*2 Corinthians 9:8* NKJV

When it comes to living out your faith, your finances can be a stumbling block—or a stepping-stone. You may be a single mom struggling to make ends meet, a wife helping her husband plan for the family's future, a new bride learning to share financial decisions with her husband, a career woman looking for good ways to invest her salary.

Whatever your situation, God wants to help you use your resources wisely. Here are some simple tips for handling your money and becoming a more faithful steward of your resources.

Always keep your integrity. Tell the truth. Keep your promises. Take responsibility for your behavior. Be generous. These are spiritually sound virtues that never go out of style and that pay off in peace of mind.

Have an attitude of gratitude. True abundance begins with

counting your blessings. Whether you have much money or little, thankfulness makes you aware of how much you enjoy the things that really count. Health, family, friends, work you love to do, community, and fellowship with believers are treasures that can never be placed in a bank account, but they are what makes life rich. As you begin to see how much you have, you will be open to sharing with others.

Stick to a disciplined savings plan. Set a regular portion of your paycheck aside for savings. Some of that money should fund a contingency reserve of two to six months' living expenses in case of emergencies. Your major savings should be for the long term—so you'll be financially free when you are ready to retire or when you have an important life transition. Having savings available gives you peace of mind during times of unexpected trouble. It also means that you are free to say yes to unexpected job opportunities or no to uncomfortable working conditions instead of staying in the same position out of fear.

Give away a percentage of your income on a regular basis. Tithing is one form of planned giving that Christians have practiced for centuries. Ten percent off the top to your church, favorite charity, or ministry is a good way to give a portion back to God.

Invest in education. To stay competitive in the workplace, invest in lifelong learning. Take classes that will enhance or broaden your work skills. To stay vital and open-minded, explore new hobbies and interests. Invest in family vacations that help your children learn as well as have fun. You'll always be glad you enriched your life with learning opportunities.

Balance your investments. Keep some of your money in safe places such as bank accounts or certificates of deposit for easy liquidation. Consult a reputable advisor for investments. Plan for long-term investment instead of short-term gain. Invest a few dollars in safety nets, including adequate home, health, auto, and life insurance.

Stay free of debt. Consumer debt can eat up your life. It starts small, but grows and grows. If you are in debt, create a plan to pay off your debt and stick with it. If you are not in debt, pay cash as often as possible, avoid impulse purchases, and pay off the entire balance of your credit card every month.

Take advantage of savvy help. From books on finances to financial advisors, you can learn how to manage your assets more wisely. Ask friends if they can recommend a reliable accountant. Check your local library for books on money management. Whether you have money to invest or are floundering in debt, it is wise to seek out information and advice that can help you safely navigate financial waters.

Finally, remember that money is not a measure of true wealth. One of the richest men in the world, John D. Rockefeller, said, "I have made many millions, but they have bought me no happiness. I would barter them all for the days I sat on an office stool in Cleveland and counted myself rich on three dollars a week." Invest your life in something lasting: your children, your family, God's work, your community, and your highest ideals. You are your ultimate investment—don't settle for less than the very best that life has to offer.

I Will

Value my integrity above financial gain. _yes_ _no_

Trust God in times of need. _yes_ _no_

Thank God for all that I have been given. _yes_ _no_

Be willing to seek out help in sorting
out my finances. _yes_ _no_

Be generous and share the gifts God has
given to me. _yes_ _no_

Look for opportunities to give to God's work. _yes_ _no_

Ask God's guidance in money matters. _yes_ _no_

Know that personal value is not an equation
with dollar value. _yes_ _no_

Things to Do

☐ Make a list of twenty things you are grateful for.

☐ Consult a reputable financial advisor.

☐ Open a savings account.

☐ Give 10 percent of your paycheck as a tithe to God.

☐ Invest in a class that will give you new skills or experiences.

☐ Look at brochures for vacations that include learning opportunities.

☐ Pay off your debts if you are in debt.

Things to Remember

She considers a field and buys it; from her profits she plants a vineyard.

PROVERBS 31:16 NKJV

None of us lives to himself, and no one dies to himself. For if we live, we live to the Lord; and if we die, we die to the Lord. Therefore, whether we live or die, we are the Lord's.

ROMANS 14:7–8 NKJV

He who trusts in his riches will fall, but the righteous shall flourish like foliage.
—PROVERBS 11:28 NKJV

The world and all its wanting, wanting, wanting is on the way out—but whoever does what God wants is set for eternity.

1 JOHN 2:7 THE MESSAGE

By their fruits you shall know them.

MATTHEW 7:20 NKJV

How much better to get wisdom than gold! And to get understanding is to be chosen rather than silver.

PROVERBS 16:16 NKJV

Lust for money brings trouble and nothing but trouble. Going down that path, some lose their footing in the faith completely and live to regret it bitterly ever after.

1 TIMOTHY 6:10 THE MESSAGE

If a brother or sister is naked and destitute of daily food, and one of you says to them, "Depart in peace, be warmed and filled," but you do not give them the things which are needed for the body, what does it profit?

JAMES 2:15–16 NKJV

Let a man consider us, as servants of Christ and stewards of the mysteries of God. Moreover it is required in stewards that one be found faithful.

1 CORINTHIANS 4:1–2 NKJV

Tell those rich in this world's wealth to quit being so full of themselves and so obsessed with money, which is here today and gone tomorrow. Tell them to go after God, who piles on all the riches we could ever manage—to do good, to be rich in helping others, to be extravagantly generous. If they do that, they'll build a treasury that will last, gaining life that is truly life.

1 TIMOTHY 6:17–19 THE MESSAGE

If you want to feel rich, just count all the things you have that money can't buy.

—AUTHOR UNKNOWN

A man that depends on the riches and honors of this world, forgetting God and the welfare of his soul, is like a little child that holds a fair apple in the hand, of agreeable exterior, promising goodness, but within 'tis rotten and full of worms.

—MARTIN LUTHER

Meditation

Think on These Things

"In your anger do not sin!" Do not let the sun go down while you are still angry.

—EPHESIANS 4:26 NIV

Meditation is a quietly powerful way to deepen your spiritual life and draw closer to God. From the psalmist who meditated on God's law and character, to Mary, the mother of Jesus, who pondered all things in her heart , the Bible teaches the value of time spent in meditation. There are many ways to approach meditation. You can memorize passages of Scripture. You can begin or end your day with reading a devotional or writing in your journal. When you set aside time for meditation, you open your heart and your mind to the Spirit's influence.

You can meditate on Scripture. But your spiritual reading can also include great books and writers of all kinds. Spiritual reading is less about the content of what you read and more about the attitude of your heart when you read. Meditating on what you read transforms reading into an activity of love and attention. Along with the Bible, look for classics that have stood the test of time. Authors of spiritual classics from history include John Bunyan,

Brother Lawrence, John Calvin, Martin Luther, Charles Finney, John Milton, and Blaise Pascal. More modern authors include C. S. Lewis, Billy Graham, Oswald Chambers, Dietrich Bonhoffer, Mother Teresa, Dorothy Sayers, G. K. Chesterton, and Flannery O'Connor. As you read, think about what insights God might want to offer to you through the printed page and how these things might apply to your daily life.

There are many other ways to meditate. Some women keep a daily journal, writing about their activities, letting their thoughts flow out onto the page. Other women prefer a more active way to meditate, take long walks in nature and mulling over their lives. Perhaps you would enjoy taking a pocket New Testament and Psalms on a walk and meditating on a Scripture passage as you look out on the wonderful view. Go into a quiet church to pray and meditate. Memorize promises from Scripture and think about them as you do household tasks. Meditation can be as simple as making a cup of tea, lighting a candle, and sitting in a comfortable chair for a time of Bible reading.

"When you meditate, imagine that Jesus Christ in person is about to talk to you about the most important thing in the world," said François Fénelon. "Give him your complete attention." Know that God wants to speak personally to you in every moment of the day. A regular time of meditation is a way of welcoming His presence into your life.

I Will

Be open to new insight from unexpected sources
when I seek out spiritual reading.   *yes*   *no*
                                                        _____   _____

Allow God to speak to my heart by meditating on
His Word.   *yes*   *no*
                                                        _____   _____

Be still and listen to God.   *yes*   *no*
                                                        _____   _____

Contemplate the meaning in the daily events of
my life.   *yes*   *no*
                                                        _____   _____

Have a teachable heart and a childlike attitude.   *yes*   *no*
                                                        _____   _____

Leave behind expectations and come to my time of
meditation with an open mind.   *yes*   *no*
                                                        _____   _____

Nurture intimacy with God.   *yes*   *no*
                                                        _____   _____

Things to Do

- [ ] Set aside a regular time for daily meditation.

- [ ] Take your Bible or a spiritual book with you to read on a walk in the woods.

- [ ] Buy a blank notebook and begin a meditation journal.

- [ ] Create a simple home altar for worship and meditation.

- [ ] Seek out a spiritual classic, such as Brother Lawrence's The Practice of the Presence of God or Oswald Chambers's My Utmost for His Highest, to complement your Bible reading.

- [ ] Listen to Scripture tapes in the car on your way to work.

- [ ] Take a short break this afternoon for a minute of meditation and mental refreshment.

Things to Remember

This book of the law shall not depart out of your mouth; you shall meditate on it day and night, so that you may be careful to act in accordance with all that is written in it. For then you shall make your way prosperous, and then you shall be successful.

JOSHUA 1:8 NRSV

Mary kept all these things and pondered them in her heart.

LUKE 2:19 NKJV

He has made His wonderful works to be remembered; the LORD is gracious and full of compassion.

PSALM 111:4 NKJV

We know only a portion of the truth, and what we say about God is always incomplete.

1 CORINTHIANS 13:9 THE MESSAGE

Knowing isn't everything. If it becomes everything, some people end up as know-it-alls who treat others as know-nothings. Real knowledge isn't that insensitive.

1 CORINTHIANS 8:7 THE MESSAGE

Meditate within your heart on your bed and be still.

PSALM 4:4 NKJV

Spiritual reading does not mean reading on spiritual or religious subjects, but reading any book that comes to hand in a spiritual way, which is to say, listening to the Spirit, alert to intimations of God.

—EUGENE PETERSON

In the rush and noise of life, as you have intervals, step home within yourselves and be still. Wait upon God, and feel his good presence; this will carry you evenly through your day's business.

—WILLIAM PENN

Prayer

In the Presence

Call to Me, and I will answer you, and show you great and mighty things, which you do not know.

—*JEREMIAH 33:3* NKJV

Prayer is communion with the God who loves you. You can cultivate many forms of prayer: praise, worship, thanksgiving, confession, adoration, petition, supplication, intercession, and meditative prayer. When you pray you come into God's presence and discover that God has been present with you all along.

You can bring your daily cares and needs to God in prayer any time, any place. He is intimately interested in the details of your life. You can ask for His guidance in your relationships, for help in whatever your need, for provision for financial and physical needs. Prayer does not have to be elaborate or long. A quick prayer as you bandage skinned knees or cook dinner connects you with your heavenly Father in an instant. He loves your heartfelt prayers, whether you kneel to pray in church or sing worship songs as you go about your daily work.

Volumes have been written about prayer, from humble

collections of devotional thoughts to great theologies of prayer. But prayer is not head knowledge that can be accessed in the pages of a book. Prayer is connecting to the God who created you, redeemed you, and loves you. Prayer is simply talking to the God who is intimately interested in your lives. Martin Luther once said, "Pray, and let God worry." The God who holds all things together is holding you together, and prayer allows Him greater access to heal your hurts, comfort your sorrows, and bring your life into alignment with His great good will.

Jesus talked about "prayer experts" who would make great show of their prayers. They would pray in public places, always with an eye to the effect they were having on the crowds who watched them at their self-conscious devotions. "Some men will spin out a long prayer telling God who and what he is, or they pray out a whole system of divinity," said evangelist Charles Finney. "Some people preach, others exhort the people, till everybody wishes they would stop, and God wishes so, too, most undoubtedly." Jesus told you that you were not to be like that, but to be as simple as children with your Father in heaven. He told you to go into a private place for an intimate encounter with God. Jesus told you that a real relationship with God does not have to be complicated, but can grow into a loving relationship of childlike faith and trust.

There are many ways to pray. There is always, first and foremost, the simple, honest, and heartfelt cry to God. This is the ground out of which a prayer life can flower. You confess your sins and admit your need. You ask for help for yourselves, for loved ones, for your community, for the church, and for the world. You turn to God, trusting that He will provide for your daily needs, protect you from danger, and guide you into wholeness and abundance.

Over the centuries the church has prayed psalms, liturgies, and simple prayers like the Lord's Prayer. Praying the beatitudes, the parables, and the psalms slowly, phrase by phrase, can call you into some new awareness of God's goodness or show you how some attitude or quality of your life is hindering your relationship with Him. It is best to pray a few well-intentioned, deeply felt, and God-directed words.

A daily devotional can help you begin or end your day with simple prayer and reading. Create a simple home altar or light some candles to create a space for prayer. Buy a blank notebook and begin to keep a prayer journal. Set aside a regular time for prayer and meditating on God's Word. Join a prayer group. Worship on a regular basis.

Understand that praying is more than bowing your head and saying prayers. Your whole life can be a prayer. Brother Lawrence was a monk whose entire life was devoted to practicing the presence of God in every moment of every day, even as he washed pots and pans. Bernard of Clairvaux said, "Wherever you are, pray secretly within yourself. If you are far from a house of prayer, give not yourself trouble to seek for one, for you yourself are a sanctuary designed for prayer. If you are in bed, or in any other place, pray there; your temple is there."

Paul wrote: I bow in prayer before the Father.

—Ephesians 3:14 NCV

I Will

Open my heart to God in prayer.   _yes_   _no_

Remember that God loves me.   _yes_   _no_

Have a childlike attitude of trust in my
relationship with God.   _yes_   _no_

Be honest with myself and with God.   _yes_   _no_

Be aware that God is with me in my daily round.   _yes_   _no_

Worship God with my whole heart.   _yes_   _no_

Resolve to make prayer a priority in my life.   _yes_   _no_

Know that my whole life can be a prayer.   _yes_   _no_

Things to Do

☐ Set aside a regular time and a special place for prayer.

☐ Worship this Sunday with other believers.

☐ Join a prayer group.

☐ Start a prayer journal.

☐ Buy a daily devotional for morning and evening quiet times and prayer.

☐ Memorize a psalm and pray it back to God.

☐ Go to a quiet chapel and kneel at the altar for a moment of prayer.

Things to Remember

Don't fret or worry. Instead of worrying, pray. Let petitions and praises shape your worries into prayers, letting God know your concerns. Before you know it, a sense of God's wholeness, everything coming together for good, will come and settle you down. It's wonderful what happens when Christ displaces worry at the center of your life.

PHILIPPIANS 4:6–7 THE MESSAGE

Evening and morning and noon I will pray, and cry aloud, and He shall hear my voice.

PSALM 55:17 NKJV

Let us therefore come boldly to the throne of grace, that we may obtain mercy and find grace to help in time of need.
—HEBREWS 4:16 NKJV

Jesus said, "Find a quiet, secluded place, so you won't be tempted to role-play before God. Just be there as simply and honestly as you can manage. The focus will shift from you to God, and you will begin to sense his grace.

MATTHEW 6:6 THE MESSAGE

On the Sabbath day we went out of the city to the riverside, where prayer was customarily made; and we sat down and spoke to the women who met there. Now a certain woman named Lydia heard us. She was a seller of purple from the city of Thyatira, who worshiped God. The Lord opened her heart to heed the things spoken by Paul.

ACTS 16:13–14 NKJV

Give ear, O LORD, to my prayer; and attend to the voice of my supplications. In the day of my trouble I will call upon You, for You will answer me.

PSALM 86:6–7 NKJV

My soul waits for the LORD more than those who watch for the morning—yes, more than those who watch for the morning.

PSALM 130:6 NKJV

Before they call I will answer, while they are yet speaking I will hear.

ISAIAH 65:24 NRSV

Pray without ceasing.

1 THESSALONIANS 5:17 KJV

I cried to the Lord with my voice, and He heard me from His holy hill. I lay down and slept; I awoke, for the Lord sustained me.

PSALM 3:4–5 NKJV

Listen to my prayer and my request, O LORD my God. Hear the cry and the prayer that your servant is making to you.

2 CHRONICLES 6:19 NLT

O Lord, I pray, please let your ear be attentive to the prayer of your servant.

NEHEMIAH 1:11 NKJV

In the morning, prayer is the key that opens to us the treasures of God's mercies and blessings; in the evening, it is the key that shuts us up under His protection and safeguard.

—HENRY WARD BEECHER

It is possible to offer fervent prayer even while walking in public or strolling alone, or seated in your shop . . . while buying or selling . . . or even while cooking.

—JOHN CHRYSOSTOM

Fitness

The Whole Person

I hope that you are as strong in body as I know you are in spirit.
—*3 JOHN 2* CEV

The spiritual life embraces the whole person—body as well as mind and spirit. Staying fit can unlock energy, helping you maintain a positive outlook and giving you the stamina to keep up with kids, husband, job, and social life. Good eating habits, adequate rest, and consistent exercise can help keep you spiritually fit, as well as physically fit. Jesus said that you were to serve the Lord with your body as well as mind and spirit.

Exercise is especially important. Researchers have found that moderate exercise in consistent increments is more effective than extreme exercising routines. Twenty or thirty minutes of aerobic exercise four to six times a week can help you lose weight, build stamina, and strengthen your heart. It will make your clothes fit better too.

Take a brisk walk—it will help you cope with stress. Take your kids for a walk in the park, stroll with your sweetheart down a neighborhood street, or simply get off the bus a few blocks early and walk to your destination.

Easy does it—start with a twenty-minute daily walk and progressively increase the time.

Strength and resistance training is also an essential ingredient in your fitness routine. You're never too old to reap the benefits of strengthening your muscles. More and more women are adding this type of exercise to their regular workouts, as strength training has been shown to help prevent osteoporosis. No matter what your age, strengthening your muscles gives you more vitality.

Here are some tips for maintaining fitness:

- Define your fitness goals and be realistic. Don't set yourself up for failure by trying to do too much too fast.

- Exercise with a friend or take a class. It's much easier to stay motivated when you have support.

- Be consistent. It takes twenty-one days for the mind and body to create a new habit. Visualize your goals and remind yourself that consistency is the key to a new way of life.

- Reward yourself. Treats and incentives will help you reach your goals and see positive results.

When your body is fit and strong, you enjoy clarity of mind, which helps you nurture your spiritual life. Honor your body for the wonder of creation that it is. Taking care of your body is a statement of faith in the God who created you. It is a statement that you want to honor the body that He has given you as a temple of God.

I Will

Remember that my body is a temple of God, to be honored and blessed. _yes_ _no_

Be consistent in my exercise program. _yes_ _no_

Be aware of my body's needs. _yes_ _no_

Enjoy the complex and wonderful gift of the healthy body God gave me. _yes_ _no_

Think of my health as a treasure to be guarded. _yes_ _no_

Be more in tune with my body's needs, and less enamored with the images portrayed on television and in magazines. _yes_ _no_

Things to Do

☐ Go to bed early tonight.

☐ Take a long walk this week to stretch your body and renew your spirit.

☐ Buy plenty of fresh fruits and vegetables the next time you shop for groceries.

☐ Sign up for a strength training class.

☐ Make an appointment for your annual check-up with your doctor to maintain good health.

☐ Eat a piece of fresh fruit instead of a sugary, salty, or fat-filled snack.

☐ Find a fun exercise program to keep your body fit and trim.

Things to Remember

If you will listen carefully to the voice of the LORD your God, and do what is right in his sight, and give heed to his commandments and keep all his statutes, I will not bring upon you any of the diseases that I brought upon the Egyptians; for I am the LORD who heals you.

EXODUS 15:26 NRSV

They are life to those who find them, and health to all their flesh.

PROVERBS 4:22 NKJV

The way of the sluggard is blocked with thorns, but the path of the upright is a highway.

PROVERBS 15:19 NIV

Bless the LORD, O my soul, and do not forget all his benefits—who forgives all your iniquity, who heals all your diseases.

PSALM 103:2–3 NRSV

Jesus said to her, "Daughter, you took a risk of faith, and now you're healed and whole. Live well, live blessed! Be healed of your plague."

MARK 5:34 THE MESSAGE

Half the spiritual difficulties that men and women suffer arise from a morbid state of health.

—HENRY WARD BEECHER

Even the best diet combined with the most potent vitamins will never tune up your muscles the way good exercise will.

—COVERT BAILEY

Wisdom

What the Heart Already Knows

Don't fool yourself. Don't think that you can be wise merely by being up-to-date with the times.

—*1 Corinthians 3:18* The Message

Many people are knowledgeable, but few are wise. The Bible tells you what wisdom is—and isn't. "Mean spirited ambition isn't wisdom. Boasting that you are wise isn't wisdom. Twisting the truth to make yourselves sound wise isn't wisdom. . . . Real wisdom, God's wisdom, begins with a holy life and is characterized by getting along with others" (James 3:14, 16 The Message). Proverbs contrasts the wise and the foolish. "Wisdom rests in the heart of him who has understanding, but what is in the heart of fools is made known" (Proverbs 14:33).

Wisdom is the knowledge and ability to make the right choices at the right time. So how do you access wisdom for living? You need wisdom that helps you cope with your work and raise your families. Most women are juggling busy schedules and need practical wisdom for the daily round. And to lift your eyes above mundane matters, you need inspiration and wisdom from heaven, too.

The greatest wisdom comes from God. Meditating on His Word will bring you wisdom. Wisdom also comes from experience; as you mature you learn from your experience. This includes learning from your mistakes, weaknesses, and problems. Sometimes your heart knows the wisest course to take, but you may still choose a foolish path. You can often learn more from your mistakes than from your successes. Your foolish choices may lead you down a path you never planned to take, but on that path you find divine appointments, lessons in love, and wise teachers who point the way back to the high road you left behind. As compost makes the soil richer, so even weaknesses, mistakes, problems, detours, and losses can enrich your life and help you cultivate wisdom. Wisdom isn't about how smart you are, or that you always make the right choices. It's about learning to understand God's compassionate ways.

Children also show you how to be wise with their wonder, openness, and willingness to try new things. Children teach lessons in life's wisdom every day. They embrace life with a giggle, are not afraid to cry when it hurts, and look with wide-eyed wonder at the world. As an adult, you may be reluctant to be open, to learn, to make mistakes. In your quest for knowing the right answers, you may leave behind the childlike ability to be open to different ideas and new experiences. Jesus warned that unless you become like a child, you would miss the wisdom of the kingdom of God.

Here are a few thoughts on how to get in touch with your childlike wisdom.

Remember what it was like to be a little girl. What did you love? What did you hate? Did you have memorable encounters with God? How did becoming an adult woman change your beliefs and your dreams?

Be open to new thoughts and experiences without expecting to gain immediate mastery. Your society rewards you for successes and correct answers. But mistakes, missteps, and misperceptions are all part of the learning process.

Be humble, accepting the possibility that someone else can teach you something you do not know already, especially about yourself. True wisdom is not about being a know-it-all. It's about having a heart willing to learn from God, able to listen to the wisdom of others.

The seasons of life offer insight as you meditate on what you learn and experience. "Every period has something new to teach us," Benedictine sister Joan Chittister observed. "The harvest of youth is achievement, the harvest of middle age is perspective, the harvest of age is wisdom." Spend some time with older women and listen to their wisdom. You can learn how to deal with your children more wisely from women who have already raised their children. Women who have lived through some of the great challenges of their era, like the Depression, World War II, the McCarthy era, or the cultural changes of the sixties, can offer stories to inspire you as you cope with the challenges of this era.

The psalmist prayed, "Teach us to number our days, that you may gain a heart of wisdom." What the mind has yet to learn, the heart already knows. God's voice of wisdom whispers to you throughout your life, showing you the path of understanding.

I Will

Be open to new ideas.

yes   no

Seek God's wisdom and guidance.

yes   no

Enjoy hearing stories of others' experiences and what
they have learned from them.

yes   no

Be thankful for the lessons I have learned from
my mistakes.

yes   no

Realize that my failures and problems are opportunities
to grow in wisdom.

yes   no

Allow myself to learn with a childlike heart.

yes   no

Be thankful for all my life experiences.

yes   no

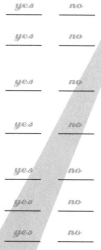

Things to Do

☐ Meditate on Proverbs, one chapter per day for a month's reading.

☐ Spend an afternoon with an older woman whom you admire.

☐ Have a conversation with a young girl and ask her what she thinks
about God.

☐ Read a book that offers practical advice on something you want to know
more about.

☐ Learn something new through a class, travel experience, or book.

☐ Join a women's Bible study group.

☐ Make an appointment with a pastor or counselor to discuss your
problems.

Things to Remember

Beloved, do not believe every spirit, but test the spirits, whether they are of God; because many false prophets have gone out into the world.

1 JOHN 4:1 NKJV

He is the source of your life in Christ Jesus, who became for us wisdom from God.

1 CORINTHIANS 1:30 NRSV

The fear of the LORD is the beginning of wisdom,
and the knowledge of the Holy One
is understanding.
—PROVERBS 9:10 NKJV

There is a spirit in man, and the breath of the Almighty gives him understanding.

JOB 32:8 NKJV

God, with your very own hands you formed me. Now breathe your wisdom over me so I can understand you.

PSALM 119:73 THE MESSAGE

If any of you lacks wisdom, let him ask of God, who gives to all liberally and without reproach, and it will be given to him.

JAMES 1:5 NKJV

Lead me in your truth and teach me, for You are the God of my salvation.

PSALM 25:5 NKJV

The wisdom that is from above is first pure, then peaceable, gentle, willing to yield, full of mercy and good fruits, without partiality and without hypocrisy.

JAMES 3:17 NKJV

The testimony of the Lord is sure, making wise the simple.

PSALM 19:7 KJV

The way of a fool is right in his own eyes, but he who heeds counsel is wise.

PROVERBS 12:15 NKJV

Wisdom is far move valuable than gold and crystal. It cannot be purchased with jewels mounted in fine gold. Coral and valuable rock crystal are worthless in trying to get it. The price of wisdom is far above pearls.

JOB 28:17–18 NLT

Accumulated knowledge does not make a wise man. Knowledgeable people are found everywhere, but we are cruelly short of wise people.

—MICHEL QUOIST

One of the greatest pieces of economic wisdom is to know what you do not know.

—JOHN KENNETH GALBRAITH

Play

You Deserve a Break Today

Our mouth was filled with laughter, and our tongue with singing. Then they said among the nations, "The LORD has done great things for them." The LORD has done great things for us, and we are glad.

—*PSALM 126:2–3* NKJV

"Child's play!" people will scoff when they want to say that a task is too easy for an adult. But in this make-a-dollar, justify-actions, bottom-line world, child's play is not as easy as it looks. Fun and play are treated with ambivalence; play is trivialized as unimportant or insignificant—certainly not promoted as being productive.

With the best of intentions you may tell yourself to work now and play later, not remembering that work sometimes takes up all the time, leaving no time for play, not realizing that you haven't played for a long, long time. Yet play is a reflection of God's ways just as much as the most serious prayer or good work. Your whole person needs the alternating rhythms of activity and rest, work and play.

God is playful. The Lord spoke to Job about how He

delights in the morning stars singing for joy and the leviathan playing in the waters. Imagine God in Genesis creating all the different animals. Can you look at a cow, a giraffe, a turtle, a monkey, or a dog without seeing the joy of creative play in their very being? Saint Gregory Nazianzen said, "For the Logos on High plays, stirring the whole cosmos back and forth, as he wills, into shapes of every kind." You who are made in God's image are meant to play—not just when you were a child, but also now as an adult. You are meant to bring childlike wonder to your games as well as to your daily work. Jesus enjoyed fellowship and relaxed into the rhythms of Sabbath rest. The legalistic Pharisees even accused Jesus of being the first-century equivalent of a party animal—the kind of man who hung around with sinners and drank too much.

If you have been too hard on yourself, too busy living in your head and giving your life over too much to work, you are missing out on the glorious gift of play. Play refreshes and renews the spirit even as it engages the body and mind. Fun is allowed. In fact, play releases your most creative thinking, helping you to break out of the box and think in unexpected ways. Artists constantly mention that a sense of play and experimentation are essential to the creative process. If you have lost play in your life, it is time now to revive the lost art. Genuine play revitalizes the spirit, refreshes the mind, and restores a sense of physical well being.

If you observe children at play, you will see that they engage themselves fully in their activity. They fully experience the moment and enjoy both physical pleasure and mental challenge of play.

How playful are you? How much time to do you allow for play or recreation in a week? A month? A year? Let your body feel the joy of movement. When was the last time you had great fun? When was the last time you really laughed hard? When was the last time you moved your body and enjoyed doing something with your whole heart?

You can play in many ways. You can actively participate in sports, fishing, camping, and hiking. You can go shopping with your friends, lunch with the girls, or try a new hairdo or lipstick. You can go to a good movie, a concert, a play, or any spectator event. You can gather a group of friends around the piano and sing or you can host a picnic with volleyball and swimming at a local park. You can tell jokes and enjoy laughter with your friends. You can retreat for a quiet hour to read a good book or for a few minutes to arrange flowers in a beautiful vase. You can grow some vegetables in your garden or try a new recipe. You can start a woodworking project or sew a new outfit. You can join family or friends to run in the park or to roller-skate.

Encourage the child within to come out and play, often, and keep in mind that playtime is productive for your well-being. Play can restore the joy in your heart, and the joy of the Lord is your strength.

Let all who take refuge in you rejoice; let them
sing joyful praises forever.
—Psalm 5:11 NLT

I Will

Be open to playful moments. *yes* *no*

Remember that play is as essential as work. *yes* *no*

Value play as a way to renew body, mind, and spirit. *yes* *no*

Look for ways to move my body in joyous
praise to God. *yes* *no*

Laugh more. *yes* *no*

See God at play in nature. *yes* *no*

Enjoy life with all of my senses. *yes* *no*

Use play to release my creativity. *yes* *no*

Things to Do

☐ Sing a happy song the next time you take a shower.

☐ Shop or go out for tea with your best friend.

☐ Put your favorite music on the stereo the next time you feel blue.

☐ Start a new project or finish a neglected one.

☐ Sleep in and have breakfast in bed.

☐ Take your husband or boyfriend on a romantic play date for two.

☐ Sign up for a class that emphasizes moving and experiencing creativity
in the body.

Things to Remember

You show me the path of life. In your presence there is fullness of joy; in your right hand are pleasures forever more.

PSALM 16:11 NRSV

The Son of Man came eating and drinking, and they say, "Look, a glutton and a wine bibber, a friend of tax collectors and sinners!" But wisdom is justified by her children.

MATTHEW 11:19 NKJV

The earth is the LORD's, and the fullness thereof; the world and they that dwell therein.
—PSALM 24:1 KJV

Jesus answered and said, "I thank You Father, Lord of heaven and earth, that You have hidden these things from the wise and prudent and have revealed them to babes."

MATTHEW 11:25 NKJV

Oh, taste and see that the LORD is good; blessed is the man who trusts in Him!

PSALM 34:8 NKJV

This is the day the LORD has made; we
will rejoice and be glad in it.

PSALM 118:24 NKJV

Blessed are the people who know the
joyful sound!

PSALM 89:15 NKJV

If you walk around with your nose in
the air, you're going to end up flat on
your face. But if you're content to be
simply yourself, you will become more
than yourself.

LUKE 14:11 THE MESSAGE

The light of the eyes rejoices the heart,
and a good report makes the bones
healthy.

PROVERBS 15:30 NKJV

Christ has set us free to live a free life.
So take your stand! Never again let
anyone put a harness of slavery on you.

GALATIANS 5:1 THE MESSAGE

Let the righteous be glad; let them
rejoice before God; yes, let them rejoice
exceedingly.

PSALM 68:3 NKJV

Jesus said, "I have told you this so that
you will be filled with joy. Yes, your joy
will overflow!"

JOHN 15:11 NLT

*It is the heart that is
not yet sure of its
God that is afraid to
laugh in His
presence.*

—GEORGE
MACDONALD

*Humor is a prelude
to faith and laughter
is the beginning of
prayer.*

—REINHOLD NIEBUHR

Joy

Sarah's Laughter

Sarah said, "God has made me laugh, and all who hear will laugh with me."

—GENESIS 21:6 NKJV

Sarah was an old woman when God went to Abraham and promised him a son. According to Genesis, Abraham "fell on his face and laughed," when he heard the promise. Sarah also laughed behind the tent door when she overheard God's promise of a son that would be born in the next year. But a year later, Sarah did give birth as God turned the joke on her. She laughed with joy and named her baby Isaac, which can be translated as "laughter." God took the tears and disappointment of a barren woman and turned them into laughter and celebration at the birth of a child.

God can also turn your sorrow into joy, your weeping into laughter. He promises this not only for this life, but in the life to come. The fulfillment you long for may come after years of waiting and hard work—or you may not know the joy you long for till you get to heaven. And sometimes joy comes unexpectedly, a surprise gift from the hand of God.

You long for happiness, which depends on circumstances; God offers you joy, which may come in spite of circumstances. Yet whenever joy from God enters your life, it feels as miraculous as that son did to old barren Sarah. The Bible promises a peace that passes understanding; it promises that those who sow in tears shall reap with joy, and that the joy of the Lord is your strength.

If you are struggling today and feel that joy has left your life, meditate on the story of Sarah. Keep in mind that God can take a barren desert and make it blossom with new life. With God all things are possible. God—not the circumstances around you or the limitations your mind perceives—is the source of your joy.

God rewards faith. Sow in faith and trust that one day you will reap in joy. Sow seeds of joy in your relationships, spending time and energy cultivating your relationships with family and friends. Tend to the homely chores that make a house a home. Be like a gardener who plants good works and positive attitudes in church, community, and career. Wait patiently like a farmer who has sown a field, letting God bring your investment to quiet fruition in His good time.

Celebrate the small victories, the daily blessings, and the unexpected moments of wonder that God sends. Let God bring you joy so you can share Sarah's laughter.

I Will

Remember that God is the source of my joy.   *yes* _____   *no* _____

Trust that God can renew my joy, even in the midst of sorrow.   *yes* _____   *no* _____

Wait patiently for the season of joy to be renewed.   *yes* _____   *no* _____

Be expectant, believing that God can do impossible things.   *yes* _____   *no* _____

Be thankful for this moment and all it offers.   *yes* _____   *no* _____

Be willing to plant seeds of future joy in my life through my daily choices.   *yes* _____   *no* _____

Be ready to bring joy to others.   *yes* _____   *no* _____

Things to Do

☐ Meditate on Sarah's story as found in Genesis 18:1–15, 21:1–8.

☐ Buy someone you love some small surprise and give it as a no-occasion gift.

☐ Buy some fresh flowers to enjoy.

☐ Make a one-dish meal and bring it to someone who would enjoy a hot meal but who may not have time or energy to make one.

☐ Send a postcard to five people who would love to hear from you.

☐ Take a long walk or do a vigorous workout—a de-stressed body is more receptive to joy.

☐ Write for twenty minutes without stopping about a time when God brought unexpected joy into your life.

Things to Remember

It's what we trust in but don't yet see
that keeps us going.

2 CORINTHIANS 5:7 THE MESSAGE

This is the day the Lord has made; we
will rejoice and be glad in it.

PSALM 118:24 NKJV

The kingdom of God is not eating, and
drinking, but righteousness and peace
and joy in the Holy Spirit.

ROMANS 14:7 NKJV

These things have I spoken to you, that
My joy may remain in you, and that
your joy may be full.

JOHN 15:11 NKJV

Restore to me the joy of Your salvation,
and uphold me by Your generous Spirit.

PSALM 51:12 NKJV

Those who sow in tears shall reap in joy.

PSALM 126:5 NKJV

Mary said to Elizabeth, "My soul
magnifies the Lord, and my spirit has
rejoiced in God my savior."

LUKE 1:46–47 NKJV

Paul wrote: I rejoice. And I will continue
to rejoice.

PHILIPPIANS 1:18 NLT

*One filled with joy
preaches without
preaching.*

—MOTHER TERESA

*Christ is not only a
remedy for your
weariness and
trouble, but he will
give you an
abundance of the
contrary, joy
and delight.*

—JONATHAN EDWARDS

Sadness

Every Tear Is Treasured

You number my wanderings; put my tears into your bottle; are they not in Your book?

—*Psalm 56:8* NKJV

A heavy heart is a load greater than you can carry alone. When your days are dark with disappointment, God understands your sorrow. He does not read you a lecture or tell you to be more cheerful. He has carried your grief and borne your sorrow. He knows your weakness and helps you.

Life has its troubles and trials. No one is immune from suffering. Sadness is a part of life. God doesn't say you won't have sorrow, but He does say that He will be with you in your sorrow and comfort you in your grief.

Perhaps you are struggling with a disappointment. A relationship has been broken and you rehearse the things you regret over and over in your mind. Or you lost your job and you have to reinvent your life while you try to pay the bills. Perhaps illness has curtailed your ability to do the things you love. You may be sad from the loss of a loved one. If you are a mother who has lost her child, there is no grief quite so deep and dark. You may be widowed or divorced, coping with loneliness and an empty heart. Though you pretend to feel positive, all you really want to do is have a good cry. God is with you in all your sorrows.

Learn to comfort yourself and allow God to comfort you. Here are some simple ways to cope during times of stress and sadness.

Take care of your health. Get some physical exercise and eat as well as you can. Make sure you get plenty of rest if at all possible.

Take a break away from the problem or trouble. Sometimes it is possible to get so focused on sadness that you can forget to look at the larger picture. Read a good book. Take a walk or go see a movie. Buy fresh flowers. Pet a puppy or hold a baby. Getting fresh perspective helps you cope with sadness.

Ask for help. In times of sadness, it's too easy to isolate yourself just when you need people the most. Take tea with a friend. Go to church and worship with others. Meet with your pastor, chaplain, or counselor. Hugs and affection support your body as well as your emotions.

Nurture your spirit through meditation, Bible reading, and prayer.

Know that God is with you in your times of sadness. He promises to never leave you or forsake you. He treasures all of your tears.

I Will

Remember that God is with me in my sadness. _____ yes _____ no

Trust that God will comfort me in times of sorrow. _____ yes _____ no

Believe the promises of God. _____ yes _____ no

Understand that tears are one way God helps you heal. _____ yes _____ no

Commit myself to taking care of my health even when I feel too sad to care. _____ yes _____ no

Rest in God's care. _____ yes _____ no

Look for the small blessings that surround me even when I am sad. _____ yes _____ no

Things to Do

☐ Make an appointment to get together with an understanding friend for a time of prayer, comfort, and encouragement.

☐ List twenty things you are thankful for today.

☐ Memorize Romans 8:28.

☐ Take a nap the next time you are feeling overwhelmed.

☐ Make a pot of homemade soup to soothe your soul and nourish your body.

☐ Make an appointment to speak to a pastor or counselor.

☐ Reread a favorite novel that comforts your heart.

Things to Remember

Praise be to the God and Father of our Lord Jesus Christ, The Father of compassion and the God of all comfort, who comforts us in all our troubles, so that we can comfort those in any trouble with the comfort we ourselves have received from God.

2 CORINTHIANS 1:3–4 NIV

I will be glad and rejoice in Your mercy, for You have considered my trouble; You have known my soul in adversities.

PSALM 31:7 NKJV

Let us therefore come boldly to the throne of grace, that we may obtain mercy and find grace to help in time of need.

HEBREWS 4:16 NKJV

This is my comfort in my affliction, for Your word has given me life.

PSALM 119:50 NKJV

He shall call upon Me, and I will answer him; I will be with him in trouble; I will deliver him and honor him.

PSALM 91:15 NKJV

My flesh and my heart faileth; but God is the strength of my heart, and my portion for ever.

PSALM 73:26 KJV

Heaven knows we need never be ashamed of our tears, for they are rain upon the blinding dust of earth, overlying our hard hearts.

—CHARLES DICKENS

The tearful praying Christian, whose distress prevents his words, will be clearly understood by the Most High.

—C. H. SPURGEON

Hopes and Dreams

If You Could Have Three Wishes

Delight yourself also in the LORD, and He shall give you the desires of your heart.

—*PSALM 37:4* NKJV

In many fairy and folk tales, the heroine is offered the opportunity to wish for her heart's desire. What would you do with three wishes? What would you wish for? The psalmist tells you that if you delight in the Lord, He will grant you the desires of your hearts. What hopes, dreams, and wishes do you wish God would grant to you?

God isn't a genie in a bottle, carelessly granting wishes with no concern for the well-being and character of the person making the wish. God wants you to partner with Him to make your dreams come true. He gives you the desire and you grow into the dream, because He has plans for you that are more wonderful and delightful than those you could imagine on your own. You might wish to be more beautiful, to have a bigger home, or to enjoy greater prosperity. But God may desire that you have more beautiful aspirations, more generous hearts, and greater awareness of the blessings you have already received.

The childlike heart loves dreams and fantasies and stories of wishes instantly granted. As you grow older, you learn that work and perseverance and trust are the way most dreams become reality. If you have a desire in your heart, a dream that you wish would become reality, here are some ways you can partner with God to make the dream come true.

First, know what you want. Articulate it and clarify it. Visualize the end result. Set specific goals to turn your dream into a reality.

Next, take the dream to God and let Him show you whether it is worthy. Continue to come to Him in prayer as you work toward the goals you have set. Any worthwhile dream grows you as you grow it. Like a seed planted in rich soil, plant your dreams in the soil of God's love and guidance.

Do the work. Realize that it may take longer than you had planned. Remember that every detour and delay is an opportunity to learn something—often a lesson that is necessary for making your dream come true. Persevere. Don't give up.

Finally, trust God to bring the dream to fruition in just the right time, just the right way. Delight in His ways and He will give you the desires of your heart. You can always trust God with your hopes, your wishes, and your dreams. Life may disappoint you, but God will never let you down.

I Will

Dare to dream big dreams because I have a big God.   yes ____ no ____

Be willing to work hard.   yes ____ no ____

Have patience with delays and problems.   yes ____ no ____

Commit myself wholeheartedly to achieving a goal
that is dear to my heart.   yes ____ no ____

Trust God to guide me.   yes ____ no ____

Trust in God's perfect timing in my life.   yes ____ no ____

Be thankful for the blessings and help I receive.   yes ____ no ____

Things to Do

☐ Answer this question in your journal: If you had three wishes, what
would you wish for?

☐ Write down a cherished goal and break it into steps to accomplish.

☐ Take the goal and the steps you wrote down and pray about what God
would have you do.

☐ Do the first item on your list of steps to accomplish.

☐ Make a collage that represents your goals and dreams.

☐ Take a class that will give you a new skill to help you reach your goal.

☐ Call some friends and set up a time to get together for mutual
encouragement.

Things to Remember

It shall come to pass that before they call, I will answer; and while they are still speaking, I will hear.

ISAIAH 65:24 NKJV

This hope we have as an anchor of the soul, both sure and steadfast, and which enters the Presence behind the veil.

HEBREWS 6:19 NKJV

We know that if our earthly house, this tent, is destroyed, we have a building from God, a house not made with hands, eternal in the heavens.

2 CORINTHIANS 5:1 NKJV

Therefore do not cast away your confidence, which has great reward. For you have need of endurance, so that after you have done the will of God, you may receive the promise.

HEBREWS 10:35–36 NKJV

The desire accomplished is sweet to the soul.

PROVERBS 13:19 KJV

Let us hold fast the confession of our hope without wavering, for He who promised is faithful.

HEBREWS 10:23 NKJV

Man finds it hard to get what he wants, because he does not want the best; God finds it hard to give, because He would give the best, and man will not take it.

—GEORGE MACDONALD

What can be hoped for which is not believed?

—SAINT AUGUSTINE

Creativity

Expressing Yourself

~~~~~~

We have different gifts, according to the grace given us.

—ROMANS 12:6 NIV

Creativity is your birthright. You are made in the image of God and when you create you honor that which is most holy and sacred within you. Creativity teacher Julia Cameron said, "Creativity is God's gift to us. Using your creativity is your gift back to God." You are meant to live creatively. Preparing a tasty new dish, planting a garden, writing a poem, restructuring a company, singing a song, decorating an office, sewing a doll's dress, building a tree house—you are born to express yourself through creative choices.

You do not have to be a fine artist or a professional musician to be creative. You can approach the whole of life creatively. You can learn to practice the art of creativity by applying lessons you learn from the ways artists approach their work. Here are a few suggestions for nurturing your creativity.

Step into the unknown with courage. Each act of creation begins with questions, chaos, and emptiness. You may have a mental picture of the finished work of art at the beginning, or just a small spark of an idea that catches your heart and connects you emotionally to the act of creation. Like any journey, whether meticulously mapped-out or launched on a whim, the creative journey starts with that first step into the unknown. Begin—and see where the work leads you.

Pay attention. Art is born in observation, awareness, and appreciation. God's creation is wondrous and complex. Your life is rich in beauty, wonder, mystery, and the commonplace miracles of life. Appreciate the details, for you will find God in them.

Trust the process. There are no wrong answers in the creative process. Don't let perfectionism keep you from creating. Process, not product, is the point of any creative activity. Often, so-called mistakes lead to a new way of seeing, a new way of approaching your work. Every experience has something to offer and is something you can apply to your creative work—and your life. "Do not fear mistakes—there are none," musician Miles Davis advised.

Practice, practice, practice. Rome wasn't built in a day, and most creative work needs time to mature. It is not by spectacular leaps that you move more deeply into your art, but by slow incremental steps. Set aside regular time for practice and nurturing your creativity. Build skills with simple daily repetition. "Practice makes perfect," may be a cliché, but it is still true, whether you want to grow a garden, paint a picture, play an instrument, or make a more creative and satisfying life.

Become a student of life. If you want to approach life more creatively, you need to expand your horizons and be open to new influences. Practice lifelong learning in the school of life. "Let a student enter art school with this advice," cautioned Robert Henri. "No matter how good the school is, his education is in his own hands. All education must be self-education."

Eric Maisel, author and a psychotherapist who counsels artists, said, "Remember the three companions of creativity: loving, knowing, doing. You can propel yourself into a creative outburst by choosing any one of the three as starting point." You can rejuvenate yourself by time spent appreciating great art, falling in love with the creations of others—loving. You can rekindle your creative spirit by learning a new skill or technique—knowing. Or you can leap right into a project, allowing the work itself to carry you along—doing.

These creative disciplines apply not only to the artistic life, but also to the spiritual life. Paul said that you are God's poem—a work of creation in progress. God was pleased with His creation of the world as chronicled in Genesis. Allowing yourself to be creative reflects a similar joy in God's creativity.

Composer Aaron Copeland said that inspiration is the antithesis of self-consciousness. Like children at play, you bring an unself-conscious joy to acts of creation, making even the simplest task an act of worship. When you lose yourself in the joy of creativity, you find God, allowing yourself to become one with what ancient hymns of the church have called the Magnum Mysterium, the Great Mystery. God created you in His image—and you reflect that image back through your creativity.

I Will

Believe that using my creativity is a gift I can offer to God.
    yes   *no*

Understand that there are lessons to be learned in both successes and failures.
    yes   *no*

Be open to new ideas.
    yes   *no*

Have the courage to start something new, learn something new, enjoy something new.
    yes   *no*

Give myself credit for trying.
    yes   *no*

Approach my life with creative passion and freedom.
    yes   *no*

Let go of my expectations and enjoy the journey as it unfolds.
    yes   *no*

Things to Do

☐ Read Genesis 1.

☐ Go to a crafts store and buy supplies.

☐ Buy a creativity workbook and do some of the exercises.

☐ Visit a museum, art gallery, or theater.

☐ Do one small creative activity today.

☐ List twenty things you enjoy doing. Do one of them.

☐ Make a creativity journal and use it on a regular basis.

Things to Remember

Make a careful exploration of who you are and the work you have been given, and then sink yourself into that. Don't be impressed with yourself. Don't compare yourself with others. Each of you must take responsibility for doing the creative best you can with your own life.

GALATIANS 6:4–5 THE MESSAGE

God created man in His own image; in the image of God He created him; male and female, He created them.

GENESIS 1:27 NKJV

Whatever you do, do it heartily, as to the Lord and not to men.
—COLOSSIANS 3:23 NKJV

We look at this Son and see the God who cannot be seen. We look at this Son and see God's original purpose in everything created. For everything, absolutely everything, above and below, visible and invisible, rank after rank after rank of angels— everything got started in him and finds its purpose in him.

COLOSSIANS 1:15–16 THE MESSAGE

Your eyes saw my substance, being yet unformed. And in Your book they were all written, the days fashioned for me, when as yet there were none of them.

PSALM 139:16 NKJV

We are His workmanship, created in Christ Jesus for good works, which God prepared beforehand that we should walk in them.

EPHESIANS 2:10 NKJV

You have an abundance of workers: stonecutters, masons, carpenters, and all kinds of artisans without number, skilled in working gold, silver, bronze, and iron.

1 CHRONICLES 22:15–16 NRSV

She makes tapestry for herself; her clothing is fine linen and purple.

PROVERBS 31:22 NKJV

If anyone is in Christ, he is a new creation; old things have passed away; behold, all things have become new.

2 CORINTHIANS 5:17 NKJV

I will sing a new song to You, O God; on a harp of ten strings I will sing praises to You.

PSALM 144:9 NKJV

The Lord said about Bezalel, "I have filled him with the Spirit of God . . . to design artistic works, to work in gold, in silver, in bronze, in cutting jewels for setting, in carving wood, and to work in all manner of workmanship."

EXODUS 31:3–5 NKJV

Every child is an artist. The problem is how to remain an artist once he grows up.

—PABLO PICASSO

To live a creative life, we must lose our fear of being wrong.

—JOSEPH CHILTON PEARCE

Family

As for Me and My House

If it seems evil to you to serve the LORD, choose for yourselves this day whom you will serve, whether the gods which your fathers served that were on the other side of the River, or of the gods of the Amorites, in whose land you dwell. But as for me and my house, we will serve the LORD.

—JOSHUA 24:15 NKJV

When Joshua gathered the tribes of Israel and said that he would serve the Lord, he was making a powerful statement. He was speaking for his family as well as himself and declaring that they were all choosing to be under the care and protection of the Lord.

As daughter and wife and mother, you want your family to be under God's protection. It is easier to see that as true if you have small children—a baby nursing in your arm, a little one asking eager questions, a toddler or preschooler exploring her mother-guarded world. But if you have older children, it is harder to protect them from the influences of others who may not serve the Lord as you know Him. But children are not the only ones who grow and change. Husband and wife change life priorities many times, sometimes in drastic ways that can tear a marriage apart. What can you do to keep your family unified? How can you serve one another, encourage godly choices, and build a strong family life that will give all of its members a solid foundation?

Rest your family foundation squarely on God. First and foremost, you are responsible to develop your own relationship with God. A mother's prayers are a powerful guard around the hearts of children. Taking time for communion with God is as essential as mopping the floors, buying the groceries, or bringing home a paycheck.

As you pray for your family, ask God

- for your family to be rooted and established in love.
- for Him to protect your family from evil.
- for Him to keep your family safe away from home and in the home.
- for your children to stay pure in thought and deed.
- for Him to provide for material needs, including lessons of giving and receiving.
- for your children to be clear thinking in selecting friends and activities.
- for wisdom and discernment in family decisions and matters of discipline.
- for Him to help each member of the family live wholeheartedly for God.

Investing in time together as a family is important. Eating dinner and doing chores together, going on family vacations, building memories as a family—these priceless, shared moments will build a solid foundation of love shared and love remembered.

Keep family rules simple and fair. Begin by prioritizing what is essential to you and your family. Kindness, taking turns, thoughtfulness, sharing, and being helpful to one another should be emphasized, not only to keep the wheels of family life running smoothly, but to help children grow into responsible adults. Be consistent and enforce safety rules no matter what. Children appreciate boundaries, and their behavior will reflect it.

Make your life an example for your children. It must be just as much "be what I am" as it is "do what I say." Always be honest. Parents should agree on discipline, and any disagreement between you and your husband should be discussed in private rather than be aired in front of the children. Show respect for your husband and honor him as head of the household. Respect your children as individuals. Show respect for yourself, as well, modeling a healthy self-image for your sons and daughters to imitate. Teach respect for other people's property. Teach your children the value of hard work. Most of all, let love rule in the heart of the family. Show your children that you value family unity by including grandparents and relatives in family activities whenever possible.

Play together as a family. Plan day-trips and family vacations. Set aside time to spend alone with each child. Get involved in family projects. Play games and share hobbies. Make sure that the TV is turned off for a family night of popcorn and games.

Teach your children lessons of love for each other and for God. Reward them for their good deeds, discipline them for their bad deeds, and love them no matter what they do. Sit together as a family in church. Create a regular family devotional time. Pray with your children before bedtime. Read aloud to them. "A godly heritage is a costly boon," wrote Andrew Murray. "Its blessing not only rests upon the children of the first family, but has often been traced in many successive generations."

I Will

Trust God to provide for and protect my family.	*yes*	*no*
Love my children no matter what.	*yes*	*no*
Be respectful of each child's individuality.	*yes*	*no*
Honor my husband.	*yes*	*no*
Enjoy the privileges and responsibilities of mothering.	*yes*	*no*
Cultivate thoughtfulness, tenderness, and empathy.	*yes*	*no*
Be positive and encouraging even when times are tough.	*yes*	*no*

Things to Do

☐ Compile a family tree and teach your children the history of their ancestors.

☐ Spend an evening going through old pictures from family vacations.

☐ Get involved in a family project that serves or helps someone less fortunate.

☐ Write each member of your family a letter sharing why you value them.

☐ Give each family member a hug.

☐ Take each of your children out to breakfast (individually).

☐ Plan a vacation together.

Things to Remember

I have known him, in order that he may command his children and his household after him, that they keep the way of the LORD, to do righteousness and justice, that the LORD may bring to Abraham what He has spoken to him.

GENESIS 18:19 NKJV

Comfort each other and edify one another, just as you are also doing.

1 THESSALONIANS 5:11 NKJV

It takes wisdom to build a house and understanding to set it on a firm foundation.
—PROVERBS 24:3 THE MESSAGE

If any widow has children or grandchildren, let them first learn to show piety at home and to repay their parents; for this is good and acceptable before God.

1 TIMOTHY 5:4 NKJV

The rod and reproof give wisdom, but a child left to himself brings great shame to his mother.

PROVERBS 29:15 NKJV

May the LORD give you increase more and more, you and your children.

PSALM 115:14 NKJV

Honor your father and your mother, that your days may be long upon the land which the LORD your God is giving you.

EXODUS 20:12 NKJV

Train up a child in the way he should go, and when he is old he will not depart from it.

PROVERBS 22:6 NKJV

Do not provoke your children, lest they become discouraged.

COLOSSIANS 3:21 NKJV

Pursue the things which make for peace and the things by which one may edify another.

ROMANS 14:19 NKJV

Our children will hear about the wonders of the Lord. His righteous acts will be told to those yet unborn. They will hear about everything he has done.

PSALM 22:30–31 NLT

A family is a place where principles are hammered and honed on the anvil of everyday living.
—CHARLES SWINDOLL

Loving relationships are a family's best protection against the challenges of the world.
—BERNIE WIEBE

Honesty

Rock-Solid Footing

He who walks righteously and speaks uprightly, he who despises the gain of oppressions, who gestures with his hands, refusing bribes, who stops his ears from hearing bloodshed, and shuts his eyes from seeing evil: He will dwell on high; his place of defense will be the fortress of rocks; bread will be given him, his water will be sure.

—ISAIAH 33:15–16 NKJV

In ancient Israel, the best defense against enemy attacks was a fortress in the rocks. A mountain fortress, like Masada, could not only be difficult for an enemy to climb and easy to defend, but often had a spring or well that provided safe water to drink during a siege. This biblical image of a fortress is often used to speak of God's protection. Many Scripture verses refer to God as a rock. Jesus spoke about building your house on a rock as opposed to building it on the shifting sand.

Choosing honesty is like building on a rock. It is a sure foundation that will keep your feet from slipping and your enemies from hurting you. God emphasizes that justice and honesty are required of those who claim to be His people. If you are to develop Christian character, honesty is not an option; it is a necessity.

The obvious place to examine your honesty is in your finances. When you receive too much change back at the store, return it. When you pay your income taxes, answer all the questions honestly. When you divide the check at a restaurant, pay your fair share. The small things add up. The next time you are tempted to be dishonest with money, ask yourself, "For what price am I willing to sell my soul?" Thirty cents? Three dollars? Thirty dollars?

Honesty is also important in relationships. You might not slander a colleague to her face. But would you drop hints to others behind her back? Do you gossip and call it "gathering necessary information"? Do you keep confidences or "spill the beans"? Honesty in dating is very difficult—where do you draw the line between wanting to make a good impression and exaggerating your assets and abilities to cover insecurity?

Complete honesty may not always be diplomatic or possible. For instance, you wouldn't tell a friend that you think the dress she's wearing is unflattering when it's too late for her to change into another dress for the occasion. But it's essential to guard your honesty and value honesty in others, especially in your most intimate relationships.

Finally, you need to be honest with God. Yes, you can say that God knows everything anyway. But if you want a real relationship with God, you have to be honest about who you are and what you feel. Honesty keeps your heart open to Him. Then you can be at rest, because you have built your life on the rock solid foundation of honesty.

I Will

Confess my sins to God. _____ yes _____ no

Believe God when He says He forgives me all my sins. _____ yes _____ no

Be honest with God about my true feelings on a matter, even if I wish I felt differently. _____ yes _____ no

Respect others by dealing honestly with them. _____ yes _____ no

Respect myself by being honest in all my dealings with others. _____ yes _____ no

Be more generous with my finances. _____ yes _____ no

Trust that God will meet my needs. _____ yes _____ no

Things to Do

☐ Go on a day or weekend retreat to examine your life.

☐ In your journal, write down five areas of your life you would like to be more honest and open about.

☐ Balance your checkbook.

☐ Answer all questions honestly on your income tax return this year.

☐ Compliment a friend when you think she looks particularly pretty or well dressed.

☐ Pay more than your fair share the next time you share a tab at a restaurant.

☐ Go to someone you have wronged and make it right.

Things to Remember

Be doers of the word, and not hearers only, deceiving yourselves.

JAMES 1:22 NKJV

Whoever comes to Me, and hears my sayings and does them, I will show you whom he is like: He is like a man building a house, who dug deep and laid the foundation on the rock.

LUKE 6:47 NKJV

We have renounced the shameful things that one hides; we refuse to practice cunning or to falsify God's word; but by the open statement of the truth we commend ourselves to the conscience of everyone in the sight of God.

2 CORINTHIANS 4:2 NRSV

God cares about honesty in the workplace. Your business is his business.

PROVERBS 16:11 THE MESSAGE

The LORD will guide you continually, and satisfy your soul in drought, and strengthen your bones; you shall be like a watered garden, and like a spring of water, whose waters do not fail.

ISAIAH 58:11 NKJV

The simple step of a courageous individual is not to take part in the lie. One word of truth outweighs the world.

—ALEXANDER SOLZHENITSYN

Our lives improve only when we take chances—and the first and most difficult risk we can take is to be honest with ourselves.

—WALTER ANDERSON

Troubles

Treasures in the Darkness

I will give you the treasures of darkness and hidden riches of secret places, that you may know that I, the LORD, who call you by your name, am the God of Israel.

—*ISAIAH 45:3* NKJV

Troubles come in all shapes and sizes. Trouble can be as small as a run in your stocking or as big as an emergency trip to the hospital. The same flat tire that made you a few minutes late for the grand opening sale at the department store could also be the few minutes that kept you from harm on the highway. When troubles come, you have a choice—to let troubles destroy you or transform you. A diamond is just a piece of coal that has undergone pressure. When you are handed a lump of coal in the form of trouble, it's an opportunity to see how God can transform it into spiritual treasure. Ugly things can become jewels reflecting the light of God, if you are willing to go into the darkness with Him and find the hidden treasure.

First, acknowledge that the trouble is real and needs to be faced. You can't ask God for help if you keep denying you have a problem. Admit that you are hurt or disappointed or angry. God can take it. He is not afraid of your honest questions, and He doesn't expect you to gloss over the problem in the name of being spiritual. Read the book of Psalms and you'll see that anger and sorrow are expressed as well as praise and thankfulness. If you can be real with God, then He can really help you.

Next, assess the situation. Ask God for wisdom and guidance. Take responsibility for what you can do in the situation. Do you need to admit a fault or ask someone for forgiveness? Do you need to make a wrong right? Is there a positive action you can take to ease the situation, relieve the trouble, or make things better? Avoid complaining. Instead, do what is in your power to do.

Perhaps there is nothing you can do right now to make things better. You may need to wait for the right timing. Or maybe something else must happen first or someone else needs to do his or her part. Sometimes a broken thing is broken and can't be fixed. Acknowledge what is out of your hands and put it into God's hands.

In the darkness, out of sight, God will use the pressures and problems to create the lovely jewel of a quiet spirit, a strengthened character, and a wiser heart. One day you will see—whether in this life or in the shining, glorious crown of glory you will behold in the next life. There are treasures to be discovered in the darkness, and troubles can be transformed into glorious victories if you can walk through them trusting God.

I Will

Trust God with my troubles.　　　　　　　　　*yes*　　*no*

Be positive when I'm tempted to complain.　　*yes*　　*no*

Be willing to take extra effort with my appearance
when I'm feeling downhearted.　　　　　　　　*yes*　　*no*

Look for the lessons my troubles can teach me.　*yes*　　*no*

Be compassionate with others who are sad, frustrated,
or troubled.　　　　　　　　　　　　　　　　*yes*　　*no*

Remember that troubles are temporary and that my
true hope rests in eternal things.　　　　　　　*yes*　　*no*

Be grateful for the small things that I normally take
for granted.　　　　　　　　　　　　　　　　*yes*　　*no*

Things to Do

☐ The next time you are tempted to complain, quickly list five things you
are grateful for.

☐ Read Psalm 42.

☐ Do one kind deed without being discovered.

☐ Write in your journal about three things that trouble you and how you
feel about them.

☐ Find and memorize a Bible verse to answer each of those three troubles
with a promise from God.

☐ Have a quiet half-hour by yourself and relax.

☐ Dress as becomingly as possible today—you'll feel better and make
others feel better, too.

Things to Remember

Cast your burden upon the LORD, and He shall sustain you; He shall never permit the righteous to be moved.

PSALM 55:22 NKJV

Do not become sluggish, but imitate those who through faith and patience inherit the promises.

HEBREWS 6:12 NKJV

Without faith it is impossible to please Him, for he who comes to God must believe that He is, and that He is a rewarder of those who diligently seek Him.

HEBREWS 11:6 NKJV

The people that walked in darkness have seen a great light; they that dwell in the land of the shadow of death, upon them hath the light shined.

ISAIAH 9:2 KJV

Everything exposed by light becomes visible, for it is light that makes everything visible.

EPHESIANS 5:13 NIV

We do not lose heart. Even though our outward man is perishing, yet the inward man is being renewed day by day.

2 CORINTHIANS 4:16 NKJV

In times of trouble, remember that God is too kind to be cruel, too wise to make a mistake, and too deep to explain himself.

—AUTHOR UNKNOWN

I would rather walk with God in the dark than go alone in the light.

—MARY GARDINER BRAINARD

Courage

The Heart of a Lion

The wicked flee when no one pursues, but the righteous are bold as a lion.

—*Proverbs 28:1* NKJV

Are you feeling bold as a lion today, ready to pounce on your problems and devour challenges with catlike grace and queenly glory? Maybe, maybe not. On most days, you may feel more like the lion's prey than the lion. *Am I a lion or lamb?* you bleat to yourself as you look danger in the eye and feel your knees knock together. Then you beat yourself up for your lack of courage, thinking that if you were a truly spiritual woman, you wouldn't be afraid.

But true courage does not come from physical prowess or a confident attitude. God is the source of your courage. Through prayer, you allow the Spirit to replenish your courage. You learn to claim the promises of Scripture, believing that God will provide the courage you need at the time you need it. Through gathering with other believers, you find encouragement and help to go on through difficult times.

True courage resides in the trembling heart that is

afraid to try but tries anyway. The one who faces a disaster and digs in, even though the mess seems hopeless, is the real hero with the heart of a lion. It takes courage to stand for your convictions when the crowd urges you to compromise. Think of Daniel in the lions' den. He knew that God would be with him, and his faith shut the mouth of a hungry lion. Courage is willing to take that first step down a path of righteousness even though you do not know where that path will lead.

Look around you. If you watch carefully, you'll see everyday heroes facing the challenges of life courageously. An alcoholic goes one more day without a drink. A single mother gets up, takes the children to school, goes to work, and comes home again at night to mouths to feed and a house to clean. A couple must choose a nursing home for a parent with Alzheimer's disease. A parent gets a call that her teenager is in trouble again. A working woman gets laid off and suddenly the steady paychecks evaporate—yet she still does her best to pay her bills on time while she is looking for the next job.

Now look at your own life. Can you see that you really do have courage, even when you are most fearful? Do you realize that you, too, may be an everyday hero? You may feel like a lamb, but God can give you the heart of a lion.

I Will

Remember that God gives me courage and strength
when I am afraid.   _yes_   _no_

Overcome my fears with faith.   _yes_   _no_

Believe God can take care of me when I am frightened. _yes_   _no_

Appreciate the courage of others.   _yes_   _no_

Face my problems with a positive attitude.   _yes_   _no_

Look before I leap, but still have the courage to leap. _yes_   _no_

Remember what it felt like when I have acted
courageously.   _yes_   _no_

Things to Do

☐ Read the biography of a courageous woman, perhaps that of Madame
Curie, Corrie ten Boom, Elisabeth Eliot, Helen Keller, or Eleanor
Roosevelt.

☐ Personalize a Bible promise for a challenging situation. Example:
"God will keep me in perfect peace in _____ because my mind is
stayed on Him."

☐ Sign up to volunteer at a hospice, a homeless shelter, or a hospital.

☐ Confront someone you have been avoiding.

☐ Try something you have been afraid to try.

☐ Take a class in self-defense.

Things to Remember

There is no room in love for fear. Well-formed love banishes fear. Since fear is crippling, a fearful life—fear of death, fear of judgment—is one not yet full formed in love.

1 JOHN 4:18 THE MESSAGE

Yet in all these things we are more than conquerors through Him who loved us.

ROMANS 8:37 NKJV

He said to me, "My grace is sufficient for you, for My strength is made perfect in weakness." Therefore most gladly I will rather boast in my infirmities, that the power of Christ may rest upon me.

2 CORINTHIANS 12:9 NKJV

Don't be bluffed into silence by the threats of bullies. There's nothing they can do to your soul, your core being. Save your fear for God, who holds your entire life—body and soul—in his hands.

MATTHEW 10:28 THE MESSAGE

I will know that you stand firm in one spirit, contending as one man for the faith of the gospel without being frightened in any way by those who oppose you.

PHILIPPIANS 1:27–28 NIV

Courage is doing what you're afraid to do. There can be no courage unless you're scared.

—EDDIE RICKENBACKER

Courage faces fear and thereby masters it. Cowardice represses fear and is thereby mastered by it.

—MARTIN LUTHER KING

Children

God's Wonderful Gift

Don't you see that children are God's best gift, the fruit of the womb his generous legacy?

—*PSALM 127:3* THE MESSAGE

Children are a gift from God. A mother's heart knows that her child—or any child—is a messenger from heaven. But you don't have to be a parent to appreciate the gifts children offer. Anyone can read God's message in the eyes of a child. A baby with ten perfect toes and ten perfect fingers and two eyes open to a wondrous new world reminds you that the world can be new for you every day. A toddler wants to touch and taste and explore—and you are reminded that God allows you to explore, but also that He sets safe boundaries until you mature in Him. Older children who are discovering books and games and friends show you that you need to be open to learning, willing to try new skills, and ready to take time to enjoy fellowship with your friends and family. Teenagers with their awkward grace and need for independence remind you that maturity takes time and patience.

How can you help your children grow into mature adults? First and foremost, give your children lots and lots of love. Let your children know that you love them. Let them know their heavenly Father loves them. Teach them to love God and His Word. Say I love you with words. Say it with hugs and affection. Say it often.

Children also need discipline. A mother needs to remember that children thrive when given strong, sure limits. Be consistent with discipline. The most important messages you convey to your children are the unspoken ones. Your good example helps children learn the difference between right and wrong. No sermon or lecture will affect children so much as watching the choices you make and knowing that they can count on you to be consistent.

Spend time together with your children. Life can be busy and complicated, but your children need to know that they come first. Mealtime, bedtime, playtime, helping with homework, attending school functions—these moments are priceless. A child grows up quickly, and before you know it the opportunity to be together has come and gone.

Finally, laugh with your kids. Let their laughter remind you that God also wants you to be a child at heart. When Jesus wanted to show His disciples how they could understand the kingdom of God, He put His arms around a child. The kingdom of heaven is filled with the joy of children's laughter—offering every busy adult a glimpse of God's love here on earth.

I Will

Appreciate God's messages of love as seen in
childhood and its wonder.

yes _____ *no* _____

Enjoy my family life or be open to sharing with other
families if I am childless.

yes _____ *no* _____

Remember that God is my Father in heaven and
loves me as His dear child.

yes _____ *no* _____

Have a sense of humor and proportion when it
comes to being around children.

yes _____ *no* _____

Treasure the passing moments and store up memories
of the good times.

yes _____ *no* _____

Be generous with love and affectionate sharing.

yes _____ *no* _____

Things to Do

☐ Give your children a beautiful gift today—your time!

☐ Have an extra cuddle time before bed tonight with a young child
or a heart-to-heart talk with an older child.

☐ Treat your children to a trip to the zoo, theme park, or walk
in the park.

☐ Ask your children what they learned in school today—and really listen.

☐ Read a story out loud.

☐ Tuck I-love-you notes in your children's lunchboxes.

☐ Ask this question of each person at the dinner table: "What is the best
thing that happened to you today?"

Things to Remember

Train up a child in the way he should go, and when he is old he will not depart from it.

PROVERBS 22:6 NKJV

Watch what God does, and then you do it, like children who learn proper behavior from their parents.

EPHESIANS 5:1 THE MESSAGE

Can a mother forget the baby at her breast and have no compassion on the child she has borne? Though she may forget, I will not forget you!

ISAIAH 49:15 NIV

Parents rejoice when their children turn out well; wise children become proud parents.

PROVERBS 23:24 THE MESSAGE

Then they brought little children to Him, that He might touch them; but the disciples rebuked those who brought them. But when Jesus saw it, He was greatly displeased and said to them, "Let the little children come to Me, and do not forbid them; for of such is the kingdom of God.

MARK 10:13–14 NKJV

I love little children, and it is not a slight thing when they who are fresh from God love us.

—CHARLES DICKENS

A baby is God's opinion that life should go on.

—CARL SANDBURG

Identity

A Very Special Person

*You are a chosen generation, a royal priesthood, a holy nation,
His own special people, that you may proclaim the praises of
Him who called you out of darkness into His marvelous light.*

—*1 PETER 2:9* NKJV

This culture likes to label and define people.
Advertisers and marketers talk about demographics,
separating people into categories according to age,
interests, and buying patterns. You were graded and
evaluated when you were in school and as an adult your
job description sorts you into department, function, and
salary level. If asked to tell someone who you are, you
could describe yourself many ways. "I am the leader of a
woman's group." "I am a wife and mother." "I am an
executive board member." You could describe yourself in
terms of race, religion, physical appearance, career
achievements, or intelligence. But the real question is not
"How do I or others define my identity?" Instead, the real
question is "How does God define my identity?"

The Bible says that your identity is in Christ, not in the
circumstances of your birth, your economic standing in
the world, or your ability to please others. This positive
identity transcends all human categories, freeing you to

live out your true calling from God. Your identity in Christ is a constant source of strength. Your hope is not in your power or righteousness or self-discipline, but in God's power working in and through you.

As a woman you may dwell on what you are not: not pretty enough, not spiritual enough, not thin enough, not a good enough wife or mother. But God sees you differently. He sees you as uniquely created and beautiful in His eyes. You are made in the image of God. You are forgiven and called in Christ.

When you claim your identity in Christ, you can have a peaceful confidence in His declaration of who you are. Circumstances may change and you may make mistakes, but God sees you as perfect and complete in His Son. This identity offers a solid foundation that gives you room to grow and change, encouraging new interests and adventures. It's large enough for a lifetime and allows you to explore who you are and what you want to become.

Your identity as God's beloved child will improve your relationships, freeing you from the need to manipulate others. You no longer have to conform to stereotypes of who and what you should be. You can revel in your own individuality and accept others' differences. You can stand for what you believe without the need to prove yourself superior to others.

Enjoy the freedom and explore the potential of your God-given identity, knowing that you are a very special person in the eyes of God.

I Will

Be confident because I know that God has called me. _yes_ _no_

Enjoy my individuality. _yes_ _no_

Invest in cultivating my gifts and talents. _yes_ _no_

Do my best and trust God with the results. _yes_ _no_

Relax in God's love instead of trying too hard. _yes_ _no_

Be empathetic to the struggles of others. _yes_ _no_

Enjoy my freedom in Christ. _yes_ _no_

Know that God thinks I am special. _yes_ _no_

Things to Do

- [ ] Tell someone why you are special today.

- [ ] Ask someone why he or she is special.

- [ ] Ask yourself why you are here on earth and write your answer in your journal.

- [ ] Write a thank-you note to someone who has encouraged you.

- [ ] Ask yourself what qualities of Christ are evident in your life.

- [ ] List ten of your strengths.

- [ ] Make a plan to maximize one of your strengths.

Things to Remember

It is better to trust in the Lord than to put confidence in man.

PSALM 118:8 NKJV

You did not choose Me, but I chose you and appointed you that you should go and bear fruit, and that your fruit should remain, that whatever you ask the Father in my name He may give you.

JOHN 15:16 NKJV

Now we see in a mirror, dimly, but then face to face. Now I know in part, but then I shall know just as I am known.

1 CORINTHIANS 13:12 NKJV

What you say about yourself means nothing in God's work. It's what God says about you that makes the difference.

2 CORINTHIANS 5:17 THE MESSAGE

It's in Christ that we find out who we are and what we are living for. Long before we first heard of Christ and got our hopes up, he had his eye on us, had designs on us for glorious living, part of the overall purpose he is working out in everything and everyone.

EPHESIANS 1:11 THE MESSAGE

To work in the world lovingly means that we are defining what we will be for, rather than reacting to what we are against.

—CHRISTINA BALDWIN

Christians have an entirely new basis for identity. This basis is a foundational reality which transcends any culture's evaluation of a person.

—BARBARA COOK

Beauty

Esther's Spa and Makeover

Each young woman's turn came to go in to King Ahasuerus after she had completed twelve months preparation, according to the regulations for the women, for thus were the days of their preparation apportioned: six months with oil of myrrh, and six months with perfumes and preparations for beautifying women.

—ESTHER 2:12 NKJV

Talk about a long time preparing for a date! It took twelve months for Esther to get ready to meet the king of Persia—and she was young and beautiful when she started! Wouldn't you like to spend a year in a spa getting gorgeous? Now that would be reveling in feminine beauty preparations: all the department-store beauty potions rolled into one fancy package. What a makeover that would be!

Of course, there was more than beauty preparation going on in the palace. Esther was in training—learning to practice the feminine arts to win a king. But Esther was more than just another female trying to win a beauty contest. Esther's character pleased the king's eunuch, and her wisdom and willingness to take a risk for God won her people's freedom and the respect of a powerful king.

Beauty is more than skin deep. Real beauty comes from the heart. First Peter 3:4 says that a woman's beauty should be that of the inner self. The ageless beauty of a gentle and womanly spirit is highly valued in God's sight. This gentle and quiet spirit is a woman who is at peace with herself and with God. What better antidote to a violent, impersonal, and competitive society than the beauty of a woman whose peaceful spirit blesses everyone she meets?

A woman who is at home in her own skin is able to be a comfortable and compassionate companion, helping others become comfortable with themselves. Clad in casual cottons or costly silks, a woman who is confident in her femininity rejoices in the fragrances, textures, sights, and sounds of God's world. She surrounds herself and those she loves with beauty and thoughtful comforts. When you walk into the home of such a woman, you can sense a spirit of peace and sacredness immediately.

Strident voices may tell you that you are not good enough and will never measure up to today's artificial and airbrushed standards of female beauty. But you can cultivate gentle strength, love of beauty, and a quiet nurturing spirit instead of trying to fit into the world's mold. Your femininity is a gift from God, and you can enjoy being a woman at any age. By all means, enjoy the feminine arts offered to today's woman. But remember Esther's brave spirit and never forget that lasting beauty comes from a heart that is at peace with God, ready to offer a womanly touch to heal a hurting world.

I Will

Remember that lasting beauty begins in the heart.   yes   no

Stop comparing myself with others. Have a peaceful and quiet spirit.   yes   no

Enjoy my femininity.   yes   no

Be compassionate and empathetic toward others.   yes   no

Be positive and cheerful when I am with others.   yes   no

Allow God's spirit to calm my heart when I am anxious.   yes   no

Things to Do

☐ *Ask God today to reveal to you what special feminine gifts you can develop.*

☐ *Sit quietly for fifteen minutes and reflect on what God is doing in your life.*

☐ *Take a fragrant bubble bath.*

☐ *Write in your journal what makes you feel feminine.*

☐ *Place fresh flowers and lighted candles on your dining room table at dinner tonight.*

☐ *Buy something beautiful for your home.*

☐ *Buy or make something beautiful to wear.*

Things to Remember

Oh, worship the LORD in the beauty of holiness!

1 CHRONICLES 16:29 NKJV

The LORD will guide you continually, and satisfy your soul in drought, and strengthen your bones; you shall be like a watered garden, and like a spring of water, whose waters do not fail.

ISAIAH 58:11 NKJV

Let the words of my mouth and the meditation of my heart be acceptable in Your sight, O LORD, my strength and my Redeemer.

PSALM 19:14 NKJV

That you may approve the things that are excellent, that you may be sincere and without offense till the day of Christ, being filled with the fruits of righteousness which are by Jesus Christ, to the glory and praise of God.

PHILIPPIANS 1:10–11 NKJV

The LORD taketh pleasure in his people; he will beautify the meek with salvation.

PSALM 149:4 KJV

Who is she who looks forth as the morning, fair as the moon, clear as the sun, awesome as an army with banners?

SONG OF SOLOMON 6:10 NKJV

Characteristics which define beauty are wholeness, harmony, and radiance.

—THOMAS AQUINAS

Beauty is God's handwriting. Welcome it in every fair face, every fair day, every fair flower.

—CHARLES KINGSLEY

Loyalty

Talk Is Cheap

Many a man claims to have unfailing love, but a faithful man who can find?

—*Proverbs 20:6* NIV

Loyalty grows out of a generous heart. Belief, and the willingness to commit to that belief, is one of the greatest gifts you can give one another. Talk is cheap, but follow-through is priceless. When a woman is loyal to the core, you'll observe that she's rich in friends and enjoys intimate and lasting relationships. In the same way, you can spot the signs of disloyalty when you see transient relationships, disillusioned friends, and disenchanted lovers. When you see a pattern of broken relationships and discarded friends, you can be pretty sure that even though the person sounds sincere, loyalty is low on the list of her priorities.

Loyalty begins with saying what you mean and meaning what you say. Easy assurances and good intentions are not enough. Are you a woman of your word? Are you willing to make a sacrifice if necessary to follow through on your promises? It's better to make no commitment than to make a false commitment. Be someone people can count on.

If you are loyal, you will try to believe the best of people. When someone slanders a friend or gossips about someone you know, the loyal choice is to believe the best before you think the worst. This is not about naive wishing, wanting to believe when you know you should be cautious. This is about assuming that your friend is innocent till proven guilty. If guilt is hiding under a smooth surface, a pattern of negative behavior will reveal itself in time. Until then, assume that you don't have all the facts and choose to believe that the person being gossiped about may be more sinned against than sinning.

Be kind and encouraging with your words and in your deeds. Bite your tongue when you are tempted to put someone down. People need encouragement more than they need critiques. You want your friends and loved ones to be able to depend on you, not only for honesty, but for your steady encouragement and belief in them.

Christ said, "I will never leave you nor forsake you." Remember that He is your most loyal friend. You can depend upon His word and trust His promises. You can take a bold stand for Him, too. Because He first loved you, you know that through His power you can be faithful to Him.

Loyalty is a sign of godly character. Treasure a loyal friend and be the kind of woman who is treasured by others for her loyal nature.

I Will

Believe the best before I think the worst of people.   yes   no

Encourage instead of criticize.   yes   no

Keep my word.   yes   no

Be kind to all I meet.   yes   no

Treasure loyalty and trust.   yes   no

Be honest with my friends.   yes   no

*Rest in God's unfailing loyalty to me,
even when I fail.*   yes   no

Things to Do

☐ *Call or write a friend to offer encouragement and to tell them how special they are to you. Be specific.*

☐ *In your journal, evaluate your ability to be a loyal friend, and list several areas where you would like to change.*

☐ *Apologize to someone in person, by phone, or in a letter to whom you have talked too harshly or judged unfairly.*

☐ *Read the book of Ruth, meditating on her loyalty to Naomi and to the God of Israel.*

☐ *The next time you hear gossip about someone you know, stand up for him or her.*

☐ *Make an anti-gossip pact with friends.*

Things to Remember

By loyalty and faithfulness iniquity is
atoned for, and by the fear of the LORD
one avoids evil.

PROVERBS 16:6 NRSV

No one can serve two masters; for either
he will hate the one and love the other,
or else he will be loyal to the one and
despise the other.

MATTHEW 6:24 NKJV

Entreat me not to leave you, or to turn
back from following after you; for
wherever you go, I will go; and wherever
you lodge, I will lodge; your people shall
be my people, and your God, my God.

RUTH 1:16 NKJV

Death and life are in the power of the
tongue, and those who love it will eat its
fruit.

PROVERBS 18:21 NKJV

What matters most is loyalty.

PROVERBS 19:22 CEV

Whoever hides hatred has lying lips, and
whoever spreads slander is a fool.

PROVERBS 10:18 NKJV

*Faithfulness in little
things is a big thing.*
—SAINT JOHN
CHRYSOSTOM

*Loyalty means not
that I am you, or
that I agree with
everything you say or
that I believe you are
always right. Loyalty
means that I share a
common ideal with
you and that
regardless of minor
differences we fight
for it, shoulder to
shoulder, confident
in one another's good
faith, trust,
constancy, and
affection.*
—KARL MENNINGER

Reaching Out

The Healing Power of Touch

When the men of that place recognized Him, they sent out into all that surrounding region, brought to Him all who were sick, and begged Him that they might only touch the hem of His garment. And as many as touched it were made well.

—MATTHEW 14:35–36 NKJV

Wherever Jesus went, people reached out to touch him. The woman with the issue of blood touched the hem of his garment and was healed. Crowds gathered around him, hoping to touch him and be healed. Jesus also reached out to touch people. He put mud on a blind man's eyes and made him see, blessed the children, touched Peter's mother-in-law and made her well, and came to Jairus's daughter's bedside and raised her from the dead.

You may not be able to cure blindness or leprosy, or raise someone from the dead. But your touch still heals. You give others a great gift when you reach out to touch them. Studies have demonstrated that physical touch is essential to human growth and well-being. It has been shown that babies in hospitals who are held and cuddled grow faster and are better adjusted than babies who are not held. What could be more comforting than a loving hug or a tender kiss? Think of family greetings at holiday time, when hugs and kisses are mingled with exclamations of "My, how you've grown!" and "It's so good to be with you again."

Reach out to those around you. When your husband is weary, discouraged by some situation at the office, make an extra effort to reach out to him with quiet undemanding affection. A backrub or shoulder massage speaks gently when words might only add to his burdens. When your children are fussy or cranky or blue, an extra cuddle (as well as a nap and some food) can make everyone feel a little better. Reach out to strangers who come to church and welcome them with a smile and a handshake. If you and your best friend have a tiff, be the first to reach out and apologize.

Be willing to reach out to others when you are in need. You need to create a circle of giving, where love is received and passed on from person to person, heart to heart. Don't stay behind self-protective walls of caution, but break down walls between people with compassion. The sympathetic touch and empathetic heart mirror the heart of Jesus, who always had time to give to those in need.

The Christmas story of Christ coming as a vulnerable baby speaks of how tenderly God wants to touch you, how far He will go to reach out to you. When you reach out and touch someone, think of it as Christ's hands touching you— Immanuel, "God is with us."

I Will

Be thankful that God is constantly reaching
out to me.   _yes_   _no_

Be alert to opportunities to reach out to others.   _yes_   _no_

Be willing to share my time and resources
with others.   _yes_   _no_

Have an open and tender heart toward others.   _yes_   _no_

Be willing to ask for and receive help from others _yes_   _no_

Have empathy for all who struggle.   _yes_   _no_

Be grateful for those who have reached out to me.   _yes_   _no_

Things to Do

☐ Sign up to volunteer at an outreach ministry that helps others in
practical ways.

☐ Give your husband or someone close to you a massage.

☐ Hug your children before they go to school and when they come
home today.

☐ Make it a point to introduce yourself to a newcomer in church
this Sunday.

☐ Visit someone in a nursing home or hospital.

☐ Call someone you haven't talked to in a long time.

☐ Write in your journal your feelings about Christ reaching out to you by
becoming one of you.

Things to Remember

She said to herself, "If only I may touch His garment, I shall be made well."

MATTHEW 9:21 NKJV

They also brought infants to Him that He might touch them; but when the disciples saw it, they rebuked them.

LUKE 18:15 NKJV

The best exercise for the heart is reaching down and lifting people up.

—ERNEST BLEVINS

He came to Bethsaida; and they brought a blind man to Him, and begged Him to touch him.

MARK 8:22 NKJV

God heals the heartbroken and bandages their wounds.

PSALM 147:3 THE MESSAGE

To ease another's heartache is to forget one's own.

—ABRAHAM LINCOLN

Comfort one another with these words.

1 THESSALONIANS 4:18 NKJV

Blessed be the God and Father of our Lord Jesus Christ, the Father of all mercies and the God of all comfort, who comforts us in all our tribulation, that we may be able to comfort those who are in trouble with the comfort by which we ourselves are comforted by God.

2 CORINTHIANS 1:3–4 NKJV

Passion

A Zest for Life

God doesn't want us to be shy with his gifts, but bold and loving and sensible.

—*2 TIMOTHY 1:7* THE MESSAGE

She's the woman with that extra glow. She only has to walk into the room and people feel better. They are drawn to her like bees to a flower, attracted by her joyous attitude and loving smile. She doesn't have to be a beautiful woman or a party girl. She's just as often a quiet person, one whom you wouldn't look at twice in a crowd. But there is something about her that draws you, warms your heart, and makes you feel better about life. She's a woman of passion, embracing life with her whole heart.

Are you a woman of passion? Do you embrace life with your whole heart? Do you love God with all your being? Or do you hang back, lukewarm and afraid to fully commit yourself to the adventure of living? Here are some ways you can embrace life and cultivate passion:

Appreciate life itself. Enjoy the details of God's creation. Rejoice in the small things as well as the large. Look around you and see how amazing and wondrous life is.

Seek out new experiences. Live your life as an adventure—never let it become a routine chore. Always be open to learning something new.

Be active, not passive. Don't let the parade of life pass you by. Join in. Don't sit back and complain. Get up out of your seat and play.

Cultivate beauty. Plant a garden. Put a rose on your desk at work. Buy that lovely scarf and wear it proudly. Go to a museum or art gallery. Take up painting or quilting. Create beauty as well as enjoying it.

Reach out to others. Smile. Get to know people who are different from you. Appreciate and enjoy the differences. Really listen when you are in a conversation. Give each person your full attention. Show affection. Be encouraging.

Add spice and color to your days. Try new dishes from exotic places. Learn new exercises to stretch your body. Break up your routine. Surprise your husband by planning a date. Give gifts for no occasion—just because. Do something fun on the spur of the moment.

Lighten up. Laugh a little more. Take to heart the biblical command to "Rejoice in the Lord always."

Be thankful for the many blessings in your life. Share some of those blessings with others.

Never be afraid to be passionate about your faith. Love God with your whole heart, mind, body, and spirit. He will be your never failing source of passion and zest for life.

I Will

Embrace life with zest and passion.   yes   no

Be open to life's surprises.   yes   no

Laugh more.   yes   no

Enjoy every moment of my days.   yes   no

Count my blessings with a grateful heart.   yes   no

Celebrate the diversity and wonder of life.   yes   no

Live my life as an adventure instead of locking
myself in a rut.   yes   no

Things to Do

☐ Sign up for a class in a subject that intrigues you.

☐ Create an original recipe.

☐ Try a new restaurant or order a new dish the next time
you go out to eat.

☐ Throw a party for all your friends—just to celebrate life.

☐ Read a travel book or adventure story.

☐ Plan a trip to an exotic locale that you would love to see.

☐ Take your husband or significant other on a surprise romantic date.

Things to Remember

With long life I will satisfy him, and show him My salvation.

PSALM 91:16 NKJV

For whoever finds me finds life, and obtains favor from the LORD.

PROVERBS 8:35 NKJV

Whether you eat or drink, or whatever you do, do all to the glory of God.

1 CORINTHIANS 10:31 NKJV

These things I have spoken to you, that My joy may remain in you, and that your joy may be full.

JOHN 15:11 NKJV

The blessing of the LORD makes one rich, and He adds no sorrow with it.

PROVERBS 10:22 NKJV

Commit your works to the LORD, and your thoughts will be established.

PROVERBS 16:3 NKJV

Paul wrote: Rejoice. Change your ways. Encourage each other. Live in harmony and peace. Then the God of love and peace will be with you.

1 CORINTHIANS 13:11 NLT

We may affirm that absolutely nothing great in the world has ever been accomplished without passion.

—GEORG HEGEL

It's not how long you live, but how well you live.

—MARTIN LUTHER KING

Worry

One Day at a Time

Do not worry about tomorrow, for tomorrow will worry about its own things. Sufficient for the day is its own trouble.

—MATTHEW 6:34 NKJV

You can be a worried person living in a troubled world. But you can also choose to be a faithful person in the world that God created, orders, and saves. Though there are real dangers, it is not worry that saves you from trouble; rather, it is a quiet faith in the God who delivers you and protects you in a time of terror.

Worry paralyzes faith, because you are assuming responsibility for things that are God's responsibility. Jesus told you not to worry, and the phrase "Be not afraid" is found over three hundred times in the New Testament. When you are worried or fearful, you focus all your attention on the danger instead of on God. Worry steals your capacity to find courage, peace, or sanity. Someone once described FEAR in an acronym: False Expectations Appearing Real. Like children picturing monsters under the bed, you create a mental movie full of monsters of lack, deprivation, trouble, and anxiety when you worry. You waste energy when you worry.

It is so easy to slip into worry. But you can choose to trust God instead. The Bible says that you are not to fear, that God is taking care of you and will provide for you. There are promises of protection and provision that remind you to cast all your cares on Him, for He cares for you. The Bible links worry with unbelief, telling you that fear is the opposite of faith. If you want to overcome worry and anxiety, you must learn to exercise your faith. When you learn to depend on God you will experience God's help and deliverance.

Worry always wants to know what's going to happen before it happens. Faith comes before the fact, not afterward. God challenges you to have faith in him. Claim God's promises, believing that God hears your requests and answers them.

You learn to trust God when you know who He is. Begin by reading His Word and thinking about it. The Bible tells you about God's character, His love, His power, and His infinite wisdom. You read stories that tell how God helped His people and delivered them from their troubles. Psalm 107 is a great worry-buster. It describes how God's steadfast love delivers you in all conditions of your life.

You strengthen your faith when you exercise it. You have to apply it to the problems you face. Every problem you worry about has a solution. You may not know the answer, but God does. Financial problems, physical illness, job troubles, relationships gone awry, family disagreements—all need to be brought to the throne of grace in prayer.

Worry is in the future tense, but faith is in the present tense. You believe in the here and now, staying with faith through the hour of trial, trusting God to help you live out this faith for yourself, for your home, for your children, for your husband, for your health problems, for your business affairs, for your community, and for your world. God promises you a peace that is beyond your understanding. You move mountains by faith, not man-made solutions.

Worry is impatient, wanting instant answers and easy solutions. But faith is patient, knowing that God's timing is not your timing, able to put the concerns in God's hands and leave them there. You must allow God to work in His way, on His timetable. Almost always it seems to take longer than you anticipated. But if you grow impatient and try to do it on your own, forcing a solution, you are taking God's work out of his hands.

Worry relies on your own limited resources. Faith relies on God's unlimited resources. You are finite. He is infinite. When you truly say "Thy will be done," you free God to provide in unexpected and delightful ways.

The next time worry starts poisoning your mind, take the faith antidote. Do one simple thing now to encourage your faith and chase anxiety away. Pray. Focus your heart on God's character and promises. Distract your one-track mind with play, companionship, or physical exercise. Center your mind with productive work instead of rehearsing your fears over and over. Take life one day at a time and let the future take care of itself.

Jesus said, "Just trust me."

—Luke 8:50 NLT

I Will

Trust that God will take care of every need.    _yes_   _no_

Focus on thoughts of God's provision instead of
my fears.   _yes_   _no_

Be thankful for what God has provided today.   _yes_   _no_

Concentrate on living in the moment instead of
worrying about tomorrow.   _yes_   _no_

Cast all my cares on God, knowing He cares for me.   _yes_   _no_

Be aware of the needs of others.   _yes_   _no_

Have a positive attitude.   _yes_   _no_

Things to Do

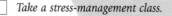

☐ List twenty-five things you thank God for today.

☐ Memorize Psalm 23 and meditate on it the next time
worry gets you down.

☐ Write a check for an I-trust-You-God offering to a favorite ministry.

☐ Have a good cry and then take a walk.

☐ Write your worries in the sand at the beach.

☐ Take a stress-management class.

☐ Call a friend and pray with her.

Things to Remember

The LORD will perfect that which concerns me; Your mercy, O LORD, endures forever; do not forsake the work of your hands.

PSALM 138:8 NKJV

Behold God is my salvation, I will trust and not be afraid; "for YAH, the LORD, is my strength and song; He also has become my salvation."

ISAIAH 12:2 NKJV

When I was burdened with worries, you comforted me and made me feel secure.
—PSALM 94:19 CEV

The LORD is on my side; I will not fear. What can man do to me? . . . It is better to trust in the LORD than to put confidence in man.

PSALM 118:6, 8 NKJV

Whoever listens to me will dwell safely, and will be secure, without fear of evil.

PROVERBS 1:33 NKJV

My help comes from the LORD, who
made heaven and earth.

PSALM 121:2 NKJV

Worry weighs us down; a cheerful word
picks us up.

PROVERBS 12:25 THE MESSAGE

We have such trust through Christ
toward God. Not that we are sufficient
of ourselves to think of anything as
being from ourselves, but our sufficiency
is from God.

2 CORINTHIANS 3:4–5 NKJV

It's wonderful what happens when
Christ displaces worry at the center of
your life.

PHILIPPIANS 4:7 THE MESSAGE

The Lord is faithful, who will establish
you and guard you from the evil one.

2 THESSALONIANS 3:3 NKJV

Do not throw away this confident trust
in the Lord, no matter what happens.
Remember the great reward it
brings you!

HEBREWS 10:35 NLT

*Feed not your spirit
on anything but
God. Cast off
concern about things,
and bear peace and
recollection in your
heart.*

—JOHN OF THE CROSS

*Care for the next
minute is just as
foolish as care for a
day in the next
thousand years. In
neither can we do
anything, in both
God is doing
everything.*

—C. S. LEWIS

Seasons

The Circle of the Year

To everything there is a season, a time for every purpose under heaven.

—*Ecclesiastes 3:1* NKJV

Life has its seasons. As the year turns and the seasons come round, you are reminded that all things have their time and place. Spring is the time of new birth and new beginnings, of seedlings pushing through the ground and small green leaves lacing the tree branches with young growth. Summer brings flowers, fruitfulness, and long lazy days with picnics and vacation and play. Fall is a time of harvest and endings, of starting school, autumn mists, and drifting leaves. Winter's cold brings a reminder of death and dormancy, yet even then the buds for next year's growth wait on the branches in anticipation of spring's warmth.

There are many seasons in your life. Newborn babies see the world for the first time and mothers also see the world anew through the innocent eyes of their children. Young girls dream about what it will be like to become a woman. As bodies change, awkward coltish adolescence matures into graceful young adulthood. A girl may fall in love, become a married woman, bear children, raise them, then see her children's children go through the same cycle again.

Through good times and bad, you can celebrate the seasons of your life. First of all, remember that God is with you in every season of your life. When the storms of sorrow tear your world apart, He is with you. When you laugh in the sunlight of happiness, He shares your joy. He walks with you in times of discouragement, waits with you for the perfect timing, and comforts you when sorrow weighs your heart to the ground.

Be ready in all seasons to see God's grace at work in your life. Know that God created this natural order of life on earth. When a season of plenty arrives, set aside the extra for the seasons when there is less to go around. Savor your moments and make memories, storing them up for future days of reverie and remembrance.

Celebrate the circle of your year. Christmas, Easter, Fourth of July, Halloween, Thanksgiving. Birthdays, weddings, anniversaries, funerals. These are all opportunities to thank God for the life He has given you, to share with others, and to savor the goodness of this moment. Even the church celebrates the seasonal round. The church year follows the circle of Advent, Christmas, Epiphany, Lent, Easter, and Pentecost, each season a remembrance of a time in the life of Christ. These remembrances and celebrations anchor your life in the love of God and the seasons of His creation.

I Will

	yes	no
Savor every season of my life.	yes	no
Know that God is with me in all the times and seasons of my life.	yes	no
Rejoice in the circle of seasons in God's beautiful creation.	yes	no
Remember the good times with a thankful heart.	yes	no
Be thankful for the lessons I've learned from difficult times.	yes	no
Enjoy my family and friends.	yes	no
Reflect on the past, rejoice in the present, and rest my future in God's hands.	yes	no

Things to Do

☐ Create a family album.

☐ Celebrate Valentine's day by giving a special gift to your sweetheart.

☐ Make a wreath or decoration out of seasonal materials.

☐ Take a day in busy December for a quiet Advent retreat.

☐ May a May Day flower basket.

☐ Write in your journal about what season of life you are experiencing right now.

☐ Be a chaperone or adult sponsor for a young people's event or retreat.

Things to Remember

He has made everything beautiful in its time. Also, He has put eternity in their hearts, except that no one can find out the work that God does from beginning to end.

ECCLESIASTES 3:11 NKJV

Here is what I have seen: It is good and fitting for one to eat and drink, and to enjoy the good of all his labor in which he toils under the sun all the days of his life which God gives him; for it is his heritage.

ECCLESIASTES 5:18 NKJV

This is the day the LORD has made; we will rejoice and be glad in it.

PSALM 118:24 NKJV

So teach us to number our days, that we may gain a heart of wisdom.

PSALM 90:12 NKJV

If you remain completely silent at this time, relief and deliverance will arise for the Jews from another place; but you and your father's house will perish. Yet who knows whether you have come to the kingdom for such a time as this?

ESTHER 4:14 NKJV

As thy days, so shall thy strength be.

DEUTERONOMY 3:25 KJV

Time lost is time when we have not lived a full human life, time unenriched by experience, creative endeavor, enjoyment, and suffering.
—DIETRICH BONHOEFFER

What is Time? The shadow on the dial, the striking of the clock, the running of the sand, day and night, summer and winter, months, years, centuries— these are but arbitrary and outward signs, the measure of Time, not Time itself. Time is the Life of the soul.
—HENRY WADSWORTH LONGFELLOW

Temptation

The Devil Can't Make Me Do It

No temptation has overtaken you except such is common to man: but God is faithful, who will not allow you to be tempted beyond what you are able, but with the temptation will also make the way of escape, that you may be able to bear it.

—*1 Corinthians 10:13* NKJV

That luscious slice of devil's food cake looks so tempting. Yet you remember: a moment on the lips, forever on the hips. If you are attracted to someone else's husband, it is easy to say you're "just being friendly" and don't really mean anything by it. When you are shortchanged at the grocery store, you make sure they make up the difference. Are you as quick to bring back the extra change when they've made a mistake in your favor? You vow not to get angry or sulky when things go wrong, and then you throw a pity party the minute life falls apart. Temptation is always with you; it's a normal part of daily life.

If you think you are immune from temptation, you deceive yourself. Just because you've managed to avoid or overcome certain "big" temptations doesn't mean you won't stumble over the more subtle temptations of life. Pride is especially tricky. There's an old saying: If you think you're humble then you are not humble because you're proud of the fact that you're being humble. Oh, temptation is very, very sneaky.

God helps you when you can't help yourself. He also helps you avoid temptation in the first place. You don't have to say "The devil made me do it!" Whether you resist temptation or give in to it, you are the one who makes the choice. And you have to live with the consequences.

How do you deal with temptation in your life? First of all, you need to be honest with yourself. A temptation by any other name is still a temptation. Acknowledge that a certain situation sets you up to be tempted and avoid that situation whenever possible. It's easy to pray "Lead us not into temptation" and then go looking for an opportunity to be tempted. Recognize the triggers and remove yourself from temptation.

Learn to say no and mean it. When you say no to a temptation, you are saying yes to yourself. Visualize your choice to forgo the tempting pleasure not as deprivation, but as a choice for a higher and better good. You are usually easier to tempt when you are feeling deprived. The temptation is presented as something that meets an unfulfilled need. Fill the empty spaces in your life with what is good and true and honorable. And always remember: You may be tempted, but the devil can't make you do it.

I Will

Pray for God's guidance and help when I am tempted. *yes* *no*

Remember and understand that when I am tempted, I
always have a choice. *yes* *no*

Trust God to deliver me when I am tempted. *yes* *no*

Remember that God will show me a way out of
temptation—or a way to avoid temptation
in the first place. *yes* *no*

Remember that everyone struggles with temptation. *yes* *no*

Be honest with myself about what tempts me. *yes* *no*

Have empathy with others who struggle with
temptation. *yes* *no*

Things to Do

☐ Write a prayer in your journal for God's help in overcoming a specific
temptation.

☐ Read and meditate on Romans 7:21–23.

☐ Say a simple "no thank you" the next time someone offers you a
tempting dish you know you should not eat.

☐ The next time you resist temptation, reward yourself with a wiser and
healthier pleasure.

☐ Ask a friend to help hold you accountable about a temptation that
troubles both of you.

☐ Develop a new habit to help you control your response to temptation.
Try counting to twenty, taking a walk, praying a simple help-me prayer.

Things to Remember

The wisdom of the prudent is to give thought to their ways, but the folly of the fool is deception.

PROVERBS 14:8 NIV

Consider it a sheer gift, friends, when tests and challenges come at you from all sides. You know that under pressure, your faith-life is forced into the open and shows its true colors. So don't try to get out of anything prematurely. Let it do its work so you become mature and well-developed, not deficient in any way.

JAMES 1:2–3 THE MESSAGE

Be on your guard and stay awake. Your enemy, the devil, is like a roaring lion, sneaking around to find someone to attack. But you must resist the devil and stay strong in your faith. You know that all over the world the Lord's followers are suffering just as you are.

1 PETER 5:8–9 CEV

It happens so regularly that it's predictable. The moment I decide to do good, sin is there to trip me up. I truly delight in God's commands, but it's pretty obvious that not all of me joins in that delight. Parts of me covertly rebel, and just when I least expect it, they take charge.

ROMANS 7:21–23 THE MESSAGE

Every temptation is great or small according as the man is.

—JEREMY TAYLOR

My temptations have been my masters in divinity.

—MARTIN LUTHER

Security

A Place to Stand

*He will not be afraid of evil tidings; His heart is steadfast,
trusting in the LORD.*

—PSALM 112:7 NKJV

Where do you place your trust? In money? In other
people? In your education or family background or social
standing? All of these things can be swept away on the
tides of changing fortune. None of them is a solid
foundation on which to build a life. God is your only real
security.

Our one sure rock to stand on in the shifting sands of
time is God. Jesus spoke about the one who built on the
sand, and how the first storm that blew through knocked
the house down. He said that placing your security in God
was like building a foundation on solid rock that would
anchor your house of faith no matter what wind and
waves and change might come.

This is especially important to remember when you
feel most vulnerable and insecure. No security system or
police force can make you 100 percent safe. No x-ray
machine, armed guard, bank account, or government
agency can guarantee that all will be well with you. True

security has to be found in God. Ultimate safety and destiny is in Him. You can trust God's kindness and good intentions, for He always follows through on His promises. In the midst of fear and uncertainty, you can rest safely in your heavenly Father's care.

You might be worried about job security right now. God says His plan for you is larger than your job. God says you are His child, and He will take care of you. Actively put your trust in Him, one day at a time. If you are struggling with a relationship, trying to make things work out and wondering if the other person cares any more, you need to remember that God always cares and will never let you down. Let God be your security, and His faithfulness will surround you.

When you have a steady place to stand, a solid foundation that is trustworthy and sure, you can dare to take risks and try new things. You can make the effort of making dreams reality. You can reach out to others and be open once again. You can overcome your fears and move beyond your comfort zone, embracing a more adventurous and courageous life.

God promises to be with you in health and in sickness, in riches or in poverty, in good times and in bad times. He promises to provide for you and protect you and guide you. He is your sure place to stand in a shaky world.

I Will

Trust God as my true security.	*yes*	*no*
Bring my fears and worries to God.	*yes*	*no*
Be willing to move beyond my comfort zone.	*yes*	*no*
Have a positive attitude in the midst of negative situations.	*yes*	*no*
Be open to other people.	*yes*	*no*
Cultivate a peaceful, trusting heart.	*yes*	*no*
Remember that God is my protector and provider.	*yes*	*no*

Things to Do

☐ Write your worries on a piece of paper—and then burn it.

☐ Do a topical study on fear, tracing God's promises through the Bible.

☐ List your blessings, naming them one by one.

☐ Comfort someone who is afraid.

☐ Write a small check to your favorite charity.

☐ Memorize a comforting Bible verse (perhaps Psalm 27:1) to remember when you are afraid.

☐ Write in your journal about a time when you felt insecure, including how you were helped by God or others in that situation.

Things to Remember

You are of God, little children, and have overcome them, because He who is in you is greater than he who is in the world.

1 JOHN 4:4 NKJV

My Father, who has given them to Me, is greater than all; and no one is able to snatch them out of My Father's hand.

JOHN 10:29 NKJV

We may boldly say: "The Lord is my helper; I will not fear. What can man do to me?"

HEBREWS 13:6 NKJV

When you pass through the waters, I will be with you; and through the rivers, they shall not overflow you. When you walk through the fire, you shall not be burned, nor shall the flame scorch you.

ISAIAH 43:2 NKJV

The minute I said, "I'm slipping, I'm falling," your love, God, took hold of me and held me fast. When I was upset and beside myself, you calmed me down and cheered me up.

PSALM 94:18–19 THE MESSAGE

There is never a fear that has not a corresponding "Fear not."

—AMY CARMICHAEL

The cure for fear is faith.

—NORMAN VINCENT PEALE

God's Word

Bible Study for Beginners

Through these things he has given us his very great and precious promises, so that through them you may participate in the divine nature and escape the corruption in the world caused by evil desires.

—*2 Peter 1:4* NIV

The Bible is God's Word. God also speaks His Living Word to you in spirit and truth, using circumstances, the wisdom of others, and the still small voice in our hearts. But there is nothing like regular Bible study to help you build a solid foundation in your daily walk of faith. If you wish to nurture a deeper spiritual life, systematic Bible study is indispensable.

There are over 37,000 promises to be found in the Bible, as well as history, prophecy, wisdom literature, letters, and instruction. Because the sixty-six books of the Bible were written over a span of hundreds of years and in different cultures and literary forms, a good Bible handbook will help you understand the background of what you are reading, helping you get the most from the text. One or more Bible commentaries can offer further insight. Bible encyclopedias help you look things up by subject. A fine study Bible often will have some form of these resources together in the same volume.

Here are some ways to study the Bible to help you unearth the treasures contained in God's Word.

- Topical studies: Select a topic and trace it through the Scriptures. For instance, you can do a study on home, or faith, or the kingdom of God.

- Character studies: The study of various people in the Bible will reward you with rich insight into your own life. Start with a study of Esther, Sarah, or Mary and see what their stories teach you about yourself and your relationship to God.

- Book studies: These help you understand the Bible through the study of one book as a whole. Begin with the Gospel of John or one of Paul's epistles.

- Memorize verses: You can hide the promises of God in your heart when you memorize Scripture.

- Psalms: For centuries Christians have read Psalms for daily devotion. You can read a single psalm per day or buy a Psalter that breaks the psalms into a month of daily readings. There are thirty-one chapters in Proverbs, for thirty-one days of the month, too.

- Reading the Bible through in a year: There are various reading plans available to guide you through the entire Bible in a year's time.

- Chapters and important passages: Studying some

of the most beloved chapters or sections of Scripture offers you a way to access the gems of biblical literature. Here are a few of the Golden Chapters of the Bible to start with: The Beatitudes (Sermon on the Mount)—Matthew 5–7; Heaven—John 14; Women—Proverbs 31; Prosperity—Psalm 73; Love—1 Corinthians 13.

• The life of Christ: Read through the four Gospels, or start with the Gospel of John to understand the birth, life, death, and resurrection of Jesus Christ. This is the life that is the fulfillment of all of the Scriptures. There is no substitute for reading the words of Christ for yourself, so that He can speak directly to your heart.

You can also claim the promises found in the Bible. These promises are based on God's character, not on human abilities, so you can depend on them. Bible promises offer you bite-size portions of Scripture to make your own, personalizing them for your life situation. You can search out a particular promise for a particular need, such as those promises you find in this book. Write the Bible promise down in your journal and write about the situation you want to apply this promise to. Write the promise on a 3 x 5 index card and post it over your mirror so you will see it every morning when you are putting on your makeup. Memorize the promise so that you carry it in your heart. Pray the promise back to God as an affirmation of faith. Be sure to record God's answers to your prayers in your journal so you can trace your growth in understanding and applying God's word.

I Will

Seek God's wisdom for my life in the Bible.   *yes* ____   *no* ____

Listen to His guidance through circumstances, people,
my intuition, and His written Word.   *yes* ____   *no* ____

Resolve to study the Bible on a regular basis.   *yes* ____   *no* ____

Make spiritual growth a priority in my life.   *yes* ____   *no* ____

Be open to new ways of understanding my relationship
with God.   *yes* ____   *no* ____

Nurture my spirit with prayer and Bible study.   *yes* ____   *no* ____

Trust God to guide me to the right resources for
spiritual understanding.   *yes* ____   *no* ____

Things to Do

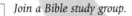

☐ Buy a good study Bible.

☐ Do a topical study on the Word of God.

☐ Start a Bible study journal.

☐ Join a Bible study group.

☐ Learn how to use a concordance, a Bible dictionary, and a Bible
commentary.

☐ Call a friend and set up a regular study time together.

☐ Memorize a meaningful section of Scripture (such as Luke 1:46–55,
the Magnificat).

Things to Remember

This Book of the Law shall not depart from your mouth, but you shall meditate in it day and night, that you may observe to do according to all that is written in it. For then you will make your way prosperous, and then you will have good success.

JOSHUA 1:8 NKJV

Let us hold fast the confession of our hope without wavering, for He who promised is faithful.

HEBREWS 10:23 NKJV

Jesus said to those Jews who believed Him, "If you abide in My word, you are my disciples indeed."

—JOHN 8:31 NKJV

Every word of God is pure; He is a shield to those that put their trust in Him.

PROVERBS 30:5 NKJV

Your word is a lamp to my feet and a light to my path.

PSALM 119:105 NKJV

The law of the LORD is perfect, converting the soul; the testimony of the LORD is sure, making wise the simple.

PSALM 19:7 NKJV

Whatever God has promised gets stamped with the Yes of Jesus.

2 CORINTHIANS 1:20 THE MESSAGE

Man does not live by bread alone, but by every word that comes from the mouth of the LORD.

DEUTERONOMY 8:3 NRSV

Your testimonies are my delight and my counselors.

PSALM 119:24 NKJV

All Scripture is given by inspiration of God, and is profitable for doctrine, for reproof, for correction, for instruction in righteousness, that the man of God may be complete, thoroughly equipped for every good work.

2 TIMOTHY 3:16 NKJV

Jesus said, "The scriptures say, 'People need more than bread for their life; they must feed on every word of God.'"

MATTHEW 4:4 NLT

Jesus said, "Even more blessed are all who hear the word of God and put it into practice."

LUKE 11:28 NLT

The Bible is alive, it speaks to me; it has hands, it lays hold on me.

—MARTIN LUTHER

Men turn this way and that in their search for new sources of comfort and inspiration, but the enduring truths are to be found in the Word of God.

—ELIZABETH, THE QUEEN MOTHER

Work

Willing Hands and Hearts

She seeks wool and flax, and willingly works with her hands.
—*PROVERBS 31:13* NKJV

True success is finding good work that allows you to develop your God-given talents and serve others. Work offers a place for community and service. Work pays the bills, nurtures the family, tends the garden, keeps the home, develops the skills, and offers a place to grow in creativity and service. It takes a lot of work to develop a career, raise a family, make a home, and create a fulfilling life.

One of the first things you need to decide is what you want to be doing for meaningful work. This is easier said than done. While some children know from an early age that they want to be a doctor, an astronaut, or a scientist, you may have had to struggle to figure out what your gifts and talents are. If you are happy in your chosen job or field, congratulations! But if you are working at a job that seems unfulfilling and stultifying, you need to do some personal archaeology to uncover the hidden treasures of talents you may not even know are there—and then find a better way to use them. There are many books, courses, and counselors available to help you with researching career options.

But meaningful work isn't limited to something you do for a paycheck. Being a mother is probably the most demanding work a woman can do, making any day job look simple in comparison. A hobby like music or gardening takes work and concentration as well. Life is more meaningful when you work with willing hands and hearts.

As a woman, you balance work and family differently in different seasons of your life. Financial necessity drives some of you into the workplace when you might rather be home with children. Many young women today are finding creative ways to have a career at home. Women are also reinventing the workplace, bringing feminine ways of relating and managing into the business mix.

Whatever your work, your days are probably very busy. Here are couple of tips to make your workday easier:

Get organized: It's distracting and frustrating to work in constant chaos. Organizing your workspace will pay dividends in time saved.

Set goals: Don't allow yourself to drift along without some sort of plan. You don't have to create a rigid set of goals to micromanage your days, but it helps to have a clear understanding of where you'd like to be in the next week, month, or year. Personal goals enable you to steer your own course instead of allow others to rock your boat.

I Will

Trust God to bless my labors.

yes ___ _no_ ___

Do my best work.

yes ___ _no_ ___

Be persistent.

yes ___ _no_ ___

Get more organized.

yes ___ _no_ ___

Have a positive attitude about my work.

yes ___ _no_ ___

Seek ways to constantly improve my work.

yes ___ _no_ ___

Cultivate a willing heart and willing hands for God's
work in the world.

yes ___ _no_ ___

Things to Do

☐ Make a prayer list of concerns you have about your work.

☐ Write out your goals for the next week, the next month, the next year,
and the next five years.

☐ Take a class to develop a skill.

☐ Make an appointment with a career counselor.

☐ Update your résumé.

☐ Organize your workspace.

☐ Write about your ambitions, dreams, and hopes in your journal.

Things to Remember

Whatever your task, put yourselves into it, as done for the Lord and not for your masters.

COLOSSIANS 3:23 NRSV

That you may approve the things that are excellent, that you may be sincere and without offense till the day of Christ, being filled with the fruits of righteousness which are by Jesus Christ, to the glory and praise of God.

PHILIPPIANS 1:10–11 NKJV

God is not unjust to forget your work and labor of love which you have shown toward His name, in that you have ministered to the saints, and do minister.

HEBREWS 6:10 NKJV

We are his workmanship, created in Christ Jesus for good works, which God prepared beforehand that we should walk in them.

EPHESIANS 2:10 NKJV

Let him that stole steal no more: but rather let him labor, working with his hands the thing which is good, that he may have to give to him that needeth.

EPHESIANS 4:28 KJV

Work without a love relationship spells burnout.

—LLOYD JOHN OGILVIE

A dairy maid can milk cows to the glory of God.

—MARTIN LUTHER

Marriage

The Two of You

Therefore a man shall leave his father and mother and be joined to his wife, and they shall become one flesh.

—Genesis 2:24 NKJV

Marriage has its seasons, and God is with you in all seasons of your married life. If you want to strengthen your marriage together, make sure the two of you invest time with one another: to bond, to sort priorities, and to remember the reasons you got married in the first place.

A new marriage is like the spring, full of new potential. Still riding on the crest of sexual attraction and romantic love, the two of you find energy and strength in simply being with each other. It's a voyage of discovery as you start a new life together.

Then comes the fruitfulness of summer. Careers begin to flourish, and children begin to arrive. You get into a rhythm with each other, and the schedules grow busier. Like a lush fruitful summer garden, your life is filled with opportunities and demands. You buy a home, establish your family, build careers, create a social life. Make nurturing your relationship a priority. Many couples set weekly date nights when they hire a babysitter, head out the door, and have some face-to-face time over a candlelit table and side-by-side time at a movie or concert or game.

Autumn is a time of change. Whether it is the emptying nest or a change in life circumstances, this is another season for the two of you to nurture your relationship. Differences that were unnoticed in a busier time of life now appear to surprise you. Often the empty spaces left from loss or change enable you to see difficult truths that you had avoided. As you let go of who you were as a couple, you need to reinvent and reinvest in who you want to be as a couple and as individuals.

Winter seasons of sorrow come to all marriages. Loss of a parent, job changes that disrupt established life, sickness, unexpected tragedies—all take their toll on the heart of a marriage. This is often the time the two of you get down to rock-bottom spiritual issues. No longer distracted by all the activities of high summer, you see the true landscape of your marriage, your personal walk with God, and where you want to create a renewed life.

Through all seasons of a marriage, remember that even when you think you know each other, there is always something new to discover. Be committed to growth. Be prepared for change. Plan to grow together as a couple, but also plan to leave plenty of room for each of you to grow and to change as individuals.

Above all, as you set your priorities together, make God the foundation of your marriage. He is unchanging in His love, mercy, and ability to help you honor and cherish one another, find common ground in spite of differences, and renew the love in your hearts.

I Will

Honor my husband and make our relationship a
priority.   _yes_ _no_

Bring my concerns to God in prayer.   _yes_ _no_

Be open to change.   _yes_ _no_

Understand that marriage has its seasons and that
God will help you in all seasons.   _yes_ _no_

Be willing to compromise.   _yes_ _no_

Make time together a priority.   _yes_ _no_

Be committed to growth, in my marriage and as an
individual.   _yes_ _no_

Things to Do

☐ Create a mission statement for your marriage with your spouse. Post it
where you will be reminded of why the two of you want to be together.

☐ Make a commitment to worship together on a regular basis for the next
month.

☐ Make a list of three things you really appreciate about your husband.
Then tell him what those three things are.

☐ Plan a romantic date for just the two of you. Spend the evening
courting each other, creating a special time for this important person in
your life.

☐ Tuck a love note in your husband's lunch or briefcase.

☐ Turn off the TV and spend an evening together just enjoying each
other's company.

Things to Remember

It is not good that man should be alone.

GENESIS 2:18 KJV

Let the husband render to his wife the affection due her, and likewise also the wife to her husband.

1 CORINTHIANS 7:3 NKJV

Jesus said, "Not everyone is mature enough to live a married life. It requires a certain aptitude and grace."

MATTHEW 19:11 THE MESSAGE

What therefore God hath joined together, let not man put asunder.

MATTHEW 19:6 KJV

Therefore comfort each other and edify one another, just as you also are doing.

1 THESSALONIANS 5:11 NKJV

House and land are handed down from parents, but a congenial spouse comes straight from God.

—PROVERBS 19:14 THE MESSAGE

Two are better than one, because they have a good reward for their labor.

ECCLESIASTES 4:9 NKJV

Let all that you do be done with love.

1 CORINTHIANS 16:14 NKJV

We don't naturally grow together and love each other more. We tend to grow apart, to grow distant. So we have to work hard at marriage. It's the most fun work in the world, but it's still work.

—ANN ORTLUND

There is no more lovely, friendly, or charming relationship, communion, or company, than a good marriage.

—MARTIN LUTHER

Success

The Secret Formula

True success is a life well lived, in harmony with God, others, and yourself. The secret of success is being true to your heart's deepest desires, seeking the best for yourself and others. Success may mean money, power, or prestige— or it may mean more intangible rewards. Success can be found in a talent developed, a garden tended, a child loved, and beauty created.

There is no one-size-fits-all formula for success, because each person defines success differently at different times in her life. In adolescence and young adulthood a young woman might define success in popularity or grades or the ability to attract a mate. As a woman matures and marries, she may find great joy and pleasure in making a home and raising happy, healthy children. Yet she also may struggle with balancing work and family, wanting to be as successful on the job as she is at home. As children leave the nest, a woman may enter into a period of reinventing herself and redefining her relationship with her husband. Some women do not marry or have children and find fulfillment in other ways of relating in the world. Today women fly in space shuttles and run corporations. A woman can define success in any way she sees fit.

There may be no secret formula for achieving success, but these practical tips may help you reach your goals for success.

Keep a positive attitude. Look for the possibilities inherent in a difficult situation and assume the best instead of dreading the worst. Negative thoughts drain your energy and distract you from doing your best.

Set goals that you can achieve. A good goal is specific, measurable, achievable, realistic, and well timed.

Do your best and take risks. Challenge yourself to reach a little higher, try a little harder, dream a bit bigger. You often underestimate what you are able to accomplish.

Don't quit. Persistence pays off. Plans and projects usually take longer than you originally plan. It's not always the most talented who is successful, but the one who is willing to work hard and stay for the long haul.

Lighten up and have some fun. If you are too serious about achieving goals, you'll miss out on the best of life. Success means nothing if you're unhappy or too busy for family and friends.

Finally, commit your way to the Lord. He helps you remember what true success is all about. He gives you the wisdom necessary for successful living.

I Will

Commit my work to God.   _yes_   _no_

Keep a positive attitude.   _yes_   _no_

Be diligent.   _yes_   _no_

Be persistent.   _yes_   _no_

Seek to live life well.   _yes_   _no_

Look for possibilities instead of
concentrating on problems.   _yes_   _no_

Define success in my own way.   _yes_   _no_

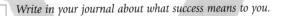

Things to Do

☐ Take a day away as a personal retreat to meditate on what is important
to you.

☐ Write in your journal about what success means to you.

☐ Make a list of successes you would like to achieve. Pray about the list.

☐ Send a thank-you note to someone who has helped or
taught or inspired you.

☐ Read a biography of someone you consider to be a success.

☐ Get together with friends and talk about your hopes, dreams, and goals.

☐ Give a donation of your time and talents to a charity or cause you
believe in.

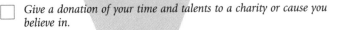

Things to Remember

I pray that you may prosper in all things and be in health, just as your soul prospers.

3 JOHN 2 NKJV

Let your light so shine before men, that they may see your good works, and glorify your Father which is in heaven.

MATTHEW 5:16 KJV

It's not possible for a person to succeed—I'm talking about eternal success—without heaven's help.

JOHN 3:27 THE MESSAGE

Whatever you do, do it heartily, as to the Lord and not to men, knowing that from the Lord you will receive the reward of the inheritance; for you serve the Lord Christ.

COLOSSIANS 3:23 NKJV

Don't look for shortcuts to God. The market is flooded with surefire, easygoing formulas for a successful life that can be practiced in your spare time. Don't fall for that stuff, even though crowds of people do. The way to life—to God!—is vigorous and requires total attention.

MATTHEW 7:13–14 THE MESSAGE

He has achieved success who has lived well, laughed often, and loved much.

—BESSIE ANDERSON STANLEY

Your success and happiness lie in you. External conditions are the accidents of life. The great enduring realities are love and service.

—HELEN KELLER

Calling

Higher Purpose

The noble man makes noble plans, and by noble deeds he stands.
—*ISAIAH 32:8* NIV

You have been called by God to become who you are meant to be in Christ. It is your decision whether or not you answer that call. Your calling is to the highest purpose. God has created and called you to bring the kingdom of heaven to earth. He has a plan for your life and if you answer His call to growth and service, He will help you become the woman He created you to be.

Don't let the world squeeze you into its own mold. You are called to be different, not because of what you do or do not do, but because of who you are and who you believe. You are called to be creative, to use your gifts and talents to make the world a better place; to be compassionate, to help one another by being the hands of God in a hurting world; to be conscientious, to do the best you can and trusting God with the rest; and to be committed, to be willing to stand for the truth even when the crowd wants you to lie.

You are a unique individual. There is no one else like

you. You have your own style, your own personality, your own quirks and preferences. You express your femininity in your own way. Some women love ruffles and roses. Other women prefer a more streamlined modern style. Some are homebodies, some are career women. You might have been a tomboy growing up, reveling in your independence and freedom. Or you might have been the little girl who preferred to follow rather than to lead, enjoying group activities where everyone encouraged each other rather than competing with one another. As you matured, you have become a unique combination of traits and interests, learning to accept the differences and appreciate diversity. God has called you to bring your unique combination of gifts and talents to a higher purpose. You are called to be like Christ.

Christ works in and through your situation and personality to bring His kingdom into the world. He gave you your gifts and talents. You don't have to be rich or famous to have an impact on your world. No one else can do what you can do, be what you can be.

Every time you make an important decision, remember that God called you. Ask yourself if this decision will serve the highest good. Remind yourself that you are somebody special in God's eyes, called to a unique and wonderful path of growth and service.

I Will

Say yes to God's calling on my life.   _yes_ ___   _no_ ___

Ask for God's guidance.   _yes_ ___   _no_ ___

Be compassionate to those who are in need.   _yes_ ___   _no_ ___

Be open and creative.   _yes_ ___   _no_ ___

Stand for the truth.   _yes_ ___   _no_ ___

Seek God's highest good in all situations.   _yes_ ___   _no_ ___

Do my best and trust God with the rest.   _yes_ ___   _no_ ___

Things to Do

☐ Create a personal mission statement.

☐ Read the biography of a famous missionary or Christian who answered an unusual call from God. (examples: Corrie ten Boom, Elisabeth Eliot, Edith Schaefer, Dietrich Bonhoeffer)

☐ Invest one hundred dollars in one of your gifts or talents.

☐ Invest one hundred dollars in someone else's ministry or talents.

☐ Send thank-you notes to five people who were a good influence on your life.

☐ Take a life-planning course.

☐ Write a simple affirmation based on your personal mission statement.

Things to Remember

To this you were called, because Christ also suffered for us, leaving us an example that you should follow in His steps.

1 PETER 2:21 NKJV

Consider your own call, brothers and sisters: not many of you were wise by human standards, not many were powerful, not many were of noble birth.

1 CORINTHIANS 1:26 NRSV

I heard the voice of the Lord saying, "Whom shall I send, and who will go for us?" And I said, "Here am I; send me!"

ISAIAH 6:8 NRSV

You did not choose me. I chose you and sent you out to produce fruit, the kind of fruit that will last.

JOHN 15:16 CEV

The gifts and the calling of God are irrevocable.

ROMANS 11:29 NKJV

I, therefore, the prisoner of the Lord, beseech you to walk worthy of the calling with which you were called.

EPHESIANS 4:1 NKJV

It's not what I do that matters, but what a sovereign God chooses to do through me.

—ELIZABETH DOLE

God has created me to do some definite service; he has committed some work to me which he has not committed to another.

—JOHN HENRY NEWMAN

Friends

Treasures from God

Agree with each other. Love each other. Be deep spirited friends.
—*Philippians 2:2* THE MESSAGE

Friendship is a gift from God. Friends laugh with you, cry with you, stand beside you. A good friend will confront you when you need to be told a difficult truth. Good friends help you grow and believe the best in you. They are treasures who enrich your life immeasurably.

Treasure your friendships. Make time to go out for lunch or tea with your female friends. It doesn't matter how old a woman is, she still needs to giggle like a teenager with trusted girlfriends. You need someone you can let your hair down with.

Make room for many kinds of friends. Longtime friends know you like nobody else. New friends help you explore new facets of who you are. Friends who share certain seasons of life often end up bonding for life. Mothers meet other mothers and share child-raising questions. Friends who share hobbies or careers help each other develop their skills and contacts. Dinner with other couples, picnics with church friends, and community get-togethers offer a kaleidoscope of friendship that enlivens you and makes life worthwhile even in the toughest times.

Friendship is a two-way street. If you want to have friends, you need to be a friend.

Be willing to reach out to other people. You never know when you'll discover a new friend.

Be loyal to your friends. Don't judge, but choose to believe the best.

Invest time in your friendships. Remember that relationships need nurturing if they are to stay healthy.

Be flexible. Allow friends room to grow and change.

Cheer each other on. Encourage one another. Be enthusiastic and supportive instead of negative and doubting.

Remember that small thoughtful acts of kindness are more important than grand gestures. Friendship is built on equality and caring for one another.

Allow friendship to have its seasons. Sometimes a friend needs more space. Sometimes your friend needs more time and attention. And sometimes you have to be willing to allow a friendship to end. Trust that as some friends leave your life, new friends will enter.

Always be honest and open with your friends. Little white lies and whispering behind someone's back will poison even the best of friendships.

Cultivate your own character so that you will be the kind of person who attracts and keeps good friends. Seek out friends who bring out the best in you. Choose and create friendships that honor God and make your world a better place.

I Will

Be thankful to God for my friends.   _yes_   _no_

Be alert to the needs of my friends.   _yes_   _no_

Lighten up, laugh, and let down my hair with
trusted girlfriends.   _yes_   _no_

Make friendship a high priority in my life.   _yes_   _no_

Be honest with my friends.   _yes_   _no_

Believe for the best and encourage the best in my
friendships.   _yes_   _no_

Appreciate the unique qualities of each of my
friends.   _yes_   _no_

Things to Do

☐ Think about what makes a good friendship and write about that in
your journal.

☐ Call your best girlfriends and make a date to go out to lunch or tea
together.

☐ Make an appointment to spend some time with a friend you haven't
seen in a while.

☐ Buy a thoughtful little gift to give a friend.

☐ Send an encouraging note to someone who needs it.

☐ Put a framed picture of you with friends on your desk at work or in a
prominent place at home to remind you of good times and good friends.

Things to Remember

A friend loves at all times, and a brother is born for adversity.

PROVERBS 17:17 NKJV

Everyone helped his neighbor, and said to his brother, "Be of good courage!"

ISAIAH 41:6 NKJV

Let all that you do be done with love.

1 CORINTHIANS 16:14 NKJV

Just as lotions and fragrance give sensual delight, a sweet friendship refreshes the soul.

PROVERBS 27:9 THE MESSAGE

Through love, serve one another.

GALATIANS 5:13 NKJV

Friends come and friends go, but a true friend sticks by you like family.

PROVERBS 18:24 THE MESSAGE

Like good stewards of the manifold grace of God, serve one another with whatever gift each of you has received.

1 PETER 4:10 NRSV

Abraham believed God, and it was imputed unto him for righteousness: and he was called the Friend of God.

JAMES 2:23 KJV

The impulse of love that leads us to the doorway of a friend is the voice of God within and we need not be afraid to follow it.

—AGNES SANFORD

The only way to have a friend is to be a friend.

—RALPH WALDO EMERSON

Silence

A Quiet Time to Hear God's Voice

Be still, and know that I am God.

—*Psalm 46:10* NKJV

In the busy rush of the modern world, you are constantly bombarded with noise. Your daily life is filled with the hum of machines and man-made technology—you swim in a sea of sound and distraction. The radio is on as you drive to work, or the television absorbs your attention when you come home tired from a busy day. You need to take time for silence, to get away for a quiet time with God and to listen to what He has to say to you.

God wants to speak to you in the silence of your heart. When your days are too crowded to spend time with Him, His heart breaks. Remember Martha and Mary? Martha was concerned with the tasks of hospitality, busy doing things for Jesus. But Mary sat at Jesus' feet, drinking in His words, just being with Him. Like Martha, it's easy to feel that you are too busy to set aside time to be quiet with God. But Jesus told anxious Martha, "Mary has chosen the better part." Mary was honored for sitting at the feet of the Lord, listening to Him.

You do not have to neglect the necessities of life to be silent before God. You can create a few minutes of quiet in the midst of a busy day. Five or ten minutes can refresh you and empower you to tackle the tasks of the day with more grace. The next time you are ironing, turn off the TV or radio and listen to the steady rhythm of the iron smoothing wrinkled fabric as an accompaniment to prayer and meditation. If you are washing dishes, be quiet before God. Retreat to a park or garden at lunch break for a few minutes of silence and contemplation. Drive to work or the store with the radio off. Create small moments of silence in your day, and you will discover that one need not make a weeklong retreat or travel to a majestic cathedral to enjoy the sweetness of quiet and peace.

If you set aside a quiet time for prayer and meditation, you'll discover the good that God has in store for those who seek him. You'll also find that you won't have as much trouble keeping up with the responsibilities of life because you will be more rested and refreshed. You need time to gather your thoughts and sort out the priorities of the day.

Your body needs quiet too. Constant noise not only wears you down mentally, it wears you down physically. The senses need time to be refreshed and renewed. The body needs quality times for rest and healing. Silence allows you to slow down, allowing your body to relax from the stress of daily distractions. If you do not take the time when you are well and have the choice, you will be forced to take the time through sickness or breakdown.

Sometimes life is so busy that it is hard to find a silent time in the day. Parents of small children often wonder when they will get a moment of quiet between the demands of family and work. When the children are napping, set aside a few minutes to renew your spirit with rest before you go back to the tasks of the day. Listen to the silence in the middle of the night.

Clear a space in your schedule for a longer silent time. Set aside a day for quiet reflection or a weekend for a silent retreat. Many churches and retreat centers offer structured opportunities for time of silence together with others. Plan for a weekend walk in the woods. Slip into a church for a few moments of silent prayer. Seek God in the sweet fragrant silence of a garden. Meditate in silence on your bed at night.

God wants to renew your spirit. Silence is a nutrient for the spirit. Think of how you felt the last time you sat in a quiet church or cathedral, or spent moments in a garden or majestic forest, contemplating the silence. Allow silence to wrap around you like a soft protecting cloak, giving you room to breathe, time to think, and space for your spirit to expand.

This should be your ambition: to live a quiet life, minding your own business and working with your hands.

—1 Thessalonians 4:11 NLT

I Will

Draw closer to God through moments of silence in my life.

yes _____ *no* _____

Remember that God wants to speak to me and wants me to take time to listen to Him.

yes _____ *no* _____

Look for times when I can add quiet and silence to my life.

yes _____ *no* _____

Remember that silence can restore and refresh me.

yes _____ *no* _____

Cultivate silent communion with God in the midst of noise and distraction.

yes _____ *no* _____

Carry the inner stillness found in silence into my busy life.

yes _____ *no* _____

Things to Do

☐ Take ten minutes in the middle of every day this week for silent reflection.

☐ Create a personal mini-retreat for an afternoon of quiet and contemplation.

☐ Ask your family to join you in having a quiet hour in your home each day: no television, no radio, no computers, no phones. Just quiet!

☐ Take a walk in a quiet garden, forest, or park.

☐ Turn the car radio or stereo off for one day and drive in silence.

☐ Get up a half-hour early tomorrow morning for a quiet time alone with God.

Things to Remember

Be silent, all people, before the LORD; for he has roused himself from his holy dwelling.

ZECHARIAH 2:13 NRSV

Are you tired? Worn out? Burned out on religion? Come to me. Get away with me and you'll recover your real life. I'll show you how to take a real rest. Walk with me and work with me—watch how I do it. Learn the unforced rhythms of grace.

MATTHEW 11:28–29 THE MESSAGE

In returning and rest you shall be saved; in quietness and confidence shall be your strength.
—ISAIAH 30:15 NKJV

Stand in awe, and sin not: commune with your own heart upon your bed, and be still.

PSALM 4:4 KJV

I have stilled and quieted my soul; like a weaned child with its mother, like a weaned child is my soul within me.

PSALM 131:2 NIV

She had a sister called Mary, who sat down in front of the Lord and was listening to what he said.

LUKE 10:38 CEV

Better one handful with tranquillity than two handfuls with toil and chasing after the wind.

ECCLESIASTES 4:6 NIV

He makes me lie down in green pastures; he leads me beside still waters.

PSALM 23:2 NRSV

If you have ears, pay attention!

MATTHEW 11:15 CEV

The LORD came and stood there, calling as at the other times, "Samuel! Samuel!" Then Samuel said, "Speak, for your servant is listening."

1 SAMUEL 3:10 NIV

The work of righteousness will be peace, and the effect of righteousnes, quietness and assurance forever. My people will live in a peaceful habitation, in secure dwellings, and in quiet resting places.

ISAIAH 32:17–18 NKJV

God is the friend of silence. See how nature—trees, flowers, grass—grow in silence? The more we receive in silent prayer, the more we can give in our active life.

—MOTHER TERESA

The miracles of the church seem to me to rest not so much on faces or voices or healing power suddenly near to us from afar off, but upon our perceptions being made finer, so that for a moment our eyes can see and our ears can hear what is there about us always.

—WILLA CATHER

Between Sloth and Sleep Deprivation

I will both lie down in peace, and sleep; for You alone, O LORD, make me dwell in safety.

—*PSALM 4:8* NKJV

Not too many years ago, Sundays were days of rest. People went to church in the morning, had a family feast together in the afternoon, and rested in the evening. People rested and did not feel guilty about it, because it was Sabbath, a day of rest. Though you may not be able to return to those quiet Sundays, the concept of Sabbath can still help you regain a better balance between work and rest.

You live in a workaholic society. You are proud that you accomplish so much, work so many hours, and produce and consume so much. But with busy schedules, cell phone, e-mails, fax machine, 24/7 days, you exhaust yourself and lose touch with the basic rhythms of creation. Even though your body and mind need rest, you often feel guilty, as if taking time to sleep, relax, and simply be a human being instead of a unit of production is a crime.

The biblical concept of Sabbath challenges the workaholic consumer society.

Sabbath is not merely a twenty-four-hour day of rest. Sabbath can be any length of time. What is important about creating your own sense of Sabbath rest is that you let go of your frantic agenda and let God take care of running the universe. Lighting candles, gathering in worship and prayer, singing songs, enjoying your children, loving your husband, sharing meals, reading Scripture, and delighting in play are all part of Sabbath rest. A nap in the afternoon sun or a brisk walk over the hills is restful to body, mind, and spirit.

If you dress up at work, dress down for a day off. If you have a job that requires uniforms or work clothes that get grimy, dressing up and going to a concert or out to dinner might be a restful and playful change for your soul. A beautiful black velvet dress and diamond drop earrings and somewhere to wear them may be as satisfying a way to play for a woman as getting into tennis whites or garden grubbies. It's about changing perspective, celebrating the beauties of your life, and taking a break from the regular routine.

Setting aside work for one day a week, or for a few moments in a day, is an act of faith, not a sign of laziness or sloth. It is an acknowledgment that you were created for rhythms of rest and work. God created for six days, and on the seventh day He rested. It is a pattern that you can use to restore balance to your own life.

I Will

Acknowledge God's design for a regular rhythm of
rest and work. <u>*yes*</u> <u>*no*</u>

Feel free to take some time off for play and
relaxation. <u>*yes*</u> <u>*no*</u>

Enjoy a departure from work day routines. <u>*yes*</u> <u>*no*</u>

Seek God in quiet moments of rest. <u>*yes*</u> <u>*no*</u>

Let God run the universe instead of trying to
control and coerce. <u>*yes*</u> <u>*no*</u>

Laugh more. <u>*yes*</u> <u>*no*</u>

Lighten up and have some fun. <u>*yes*</u> <u>*no*</u>

Things to Do

☐ Create your own Sabbath day this week.

☐ Go for a long walk in the woods or at the seashore.

☐ Spend a quiet afternoon reading a book in front of a fire.

☐ Dress up for church this Sunday.

☐ Buy tickets and go to a concert.

☐ Create an evening Sabbath ritual of lighting candles, reading
Scripture, and sharing a special meal with loved ones.

☐ Spend an hour playing with children.

Things to Remember

Jesus said, "Here's what I want you to do: Find a quiet secluded place so you won't be tempted to role-play before God. Just be there as simply and honestly as you can manage. The focus will shift from you to God, and you will begin to sense his grace."

MATTHEW 6:6 THE MESSAGE

He said to them, "Come aside by yourselves to a deserted place and rest awhile." For there were many coming and going, and they did not even have time to eat.

MARK 6:31 NKJV

I want you woven into a tapestry of love, in touch with everything there is to know of God. Then you will have minds confident and at rest, focused on Christ, God's great mystery.

COLOSSIANS 2:2 THE MESSAGE

He makes me to lie down in green pastures; He leads me beside the still waters.

PSALM 23:2 NKJV

Remember the Sabbath day, to keep it holy.

EXODUS 20:8 NKJV

Sabbath time can be a revolutionary challenge to the violence of overwork, mindless accumulation, and the endless multiplication of desires, responsibilities, and accomplishments. Sabbath is a way of being in time where we remember who we are, remember what we know, and taste the gifts of spirit and eternity.
—WAYNE MULLER

Sunday is like a stile between the fields of toil, where we can kneel and pray, sit and meditate.
—HENRY WADSWORTH LONGFELLOW

Love

Open Arms

Since you have purified your souls in obeying the truth through the Spirit in sincere love of the brethren, love one another fervently with a pure heart.

—1 PETER 1:22 NKJV

What's the first thing you think of when you hear the word *love*? Love is a large subject, impossible to contain in a few little words. You have felt the power of love. You have tasted the disappointments of love. You have sung along with love ditties on the radio and have joined in with the congregation to sing stirring hymns of God's unfailing love. Television shows and movies often confuse love with sex, while literature offers romantic love as the answer to our heart's deepest desire. Meanwhile, commercials warn you that you will never be lovable if you don't buy this deodorant or that toothpaste. You are bombarded with different definitions of what love is—and all of them seem very small when you encounter the real thing.

A woman's heart yearns for love, no matter what her age. You find love in the family as small children. Adolescence brings girlish dreams of romantic love. As you mature, you discover deeper loves: the love of a husband, the love for children, the love for your community. Encountering God's transcendent love for you introduces you to a love that embraces all these loves and more.

Love is not a spectator sport. Love requires a real commitment. You can't fake love. And when you've tasted the real thing, no substitute will ever satisfy again. When you choose to open your heart to the mystery of love, you are choosing to participate in God's plan, sharing with others and opening your arms to the revolution of love. It doesn't matter whether you fall in love with a person or encounter love in your brothers and sisters—real love always brings transformation and change into your life. When the love of God touches you, the revolution will be more profound than anything you have ever known.

Think about the impact that an encounter with real love has had on your life. Remember a time when love touched you—whether it was the first love of adolescence, the primal love of a mother for her newborn child, the love of friends or family that kept you safe in stormy times, or a spiritual encounter that revealed God's unfathomable love for you. Anything that partakes of even a small portion of the fullness of love will teach you about love.

Love's qualities include:

• Commitment: The willingness to make yourself available is part of love. You embrace the vulnerability of opening your heart to others, to God, to all the joys and sorrows of love. Love requires that you open your heart—and open your arms to the beloved.

• Compassion: Sympathy with others' suffering is part of love. You cannot be clinical and distant and still love. Love teaches you compassion, so that you want to help and heal those whom you love, those whom God loves. Have compassion for the beloved.

• Attention: Noticing and focusing your attention on the beloved, seeing things in a new perspective, is part of the transformation of love. You become aware of things you once passed over or took for granted. Gratitude and appreciation blossom when you choose to cultivate love in your life.

• Empathy: Loving imagination empathizes with the delights and defeats of others. You not only appreciate their struggles, but also desire to encourage them, creating a community of love.

• Faith: You believe that love is possible in spite of all the things that would try to convince you that love is a lie. Faith moves you beyond the darkness of cynicism and doubt into the light of love's possibilities.

• Trust: You recognize that every relationship has a higher purpose and every circumstance has meaning, even when you do not understand or when you struggle with unanswered questions. Love commands you to put your trust in God, not in your own reason or abilities.

• Surrender: When you let go of your preconceptions, love teaches the lesson of surrender. Love knocks down walls, frees you from the prison of self, and leads you into a deeply surrendered relationship to God.

If you want to understand more about love, study the Scriptures, especially the life of Christ. His life offers a beautiful picture of the Father's unfailing love for you. Say yes to love—and to God. Open your arms and embrace the mystery of love.

I Will

Open my heart to the love of God.   *yes*   *no*

Risk vulnerability.   *yes*   *no*

Honor others and respect myself.   *yes*   *no*

Empathize with others and share their joys
and sorrows.   *yes*   *no*

Cultivate love in my life.   *yes*   *no*

Embrace love's possibilities.   *yes*   *no*

Believe in the transformational power of
God's love.   *yes*   *no*

Things to Do

☐ Read about the life of Christ in the Gospel of John.

☐ Meditate on 1 Corinthians 13, the great love chapter of the Bible.

☐ Reach out and be a blessing to someone today.

☐ Write in your journal about a time when love touched you deeply.

☐ Make a list of practical acts of kindness you can do for others.

☐ Do one act of kindness anonymously.

☐ Contact family members and let them know you love them.

Things to Remember

The whole point of what we're urging is simply love—love uncontaminated by self-interest and counterfeit faith, a life open to God.

1 Timothy 1:5 the message

It is written, "What no eye has seen, nor ear heard, nor the human heart conceived, what God has prepared for those who love him"—these things God has revealed to us through the Spirit.

1 Corinthians 2:9 nrsv

I will mention the lovingkindnesses of the Lord and the praises of the Lord.
—Isaiah 63:7 nkjv

Love from the center of who you are; don't fake it. Run for dear life from evil, hold on for dear life to good. Be good friends who love deeply.

Romans 12:9–10 the message

He who has My commandments and keeps them, it is he who loves Me. And he who loves Me will be loved by my Father, and I will love him and manifest Myself to him.

John 14:21 nkjv

Therefore know that the Lord your God, He is God, the faithful God who keeps covenant and mercy for a thousand generations with those who love Him and keep His commandments.

DEUTERONOMY 7:9 NKJV

You shall not take vengeance or bear a grudge against any of your people, but you shall love your neighbor as yourself: I am the Lord.

LEVITICUS 19:18 NRSV

Love does no harm to a neighbor; therefore love is the fulfillment of the law.

ROMANS 13:10 NKJV

This commandment we have from Him: that he who loves God must love his brother also.

1 JOHN 4:21 NKJV

Now abide faith, hope, and love, these three; but the greatest of these is love.

1 CORINTHIANS 13:6 NKJV

Jesus said, "Just as I have loved you, you should love each other. Your love for one another will prove to the world that you are my disciples."

JOHN 13:34–35 NLT

A loving heart is the truest wisdom.

—CHARLES DICKENS

Love has the power to give in a moment what toil can scarcely reach in an age.

—GOETHE

Envy

Green Eyes

A sound heart is life to the body, but envy is rotten to the bones.
—*Proverbs 14:30* NKJV

Envy has jealous green eyes. You know how it feels to be envious. The lonely teenage girl with acne envies the popular cheerleader with creamy clear skin. A young mother envies her single friend's freedom, while the single woman envies the married woman's love and security. Passed over for a promotion, an office worker envies another's easy climb to the top. Most people envy the accomplishments, looks, successes, and loves of others. Envy flashes its jade eyes when it sees someone who has what you want.

Envy and jealousy can offer clues to who you'd like to be and what you'd like to change about yourself. Here's a simple exercise to help you transform envy into a self-help tool: Make a list of everyone you envy. Write down who they are, what qualities you envy, and an action step you can take to develop that quality in your own life. Be as specific and accurate as you can. If you envy someone her svelte figure, list exercising more and eating better for your action antidote. If someone's beautiful voice makes you wish you could sing, perhaps you should invest in voice lessons. If you envy how much love another woman has in her life, cultivate love in your own life. The biggest changes begin with small actions. A positive action is a powerful antidote to a negative emotion.

Envy can keep you stuck. Or it can be a catalyst for personal growth. You can choose to become more compassionate and empathetic. Though you may feel insecure next to someone else, you need to understand that envy colors the way you see the other person. Remember that you only see the outside, not the inside. She may seem secure and confident to you, but if you could look past the surface, you might discover she's as envious of you as you are of her. You don't know someone's struggles. You don't know their hidden pain. Feelings of envy and jealousy are reminders to look for what lies beneath surface appearances. Perhaps the woman you envy is more like you than you realize, deep down inside.

When the snakebite of envy's poison clouds your vision, take an action antidote. Cultivate the qualities you desire in your own life. Learn to look past surface appearances. Become more generous and compassionate to others. Then the cold jade green of envy will turn into the new leaf green of personal growth, enabling you to see the world with clearer vision.

I Will

Remember to use my feelings of envy as a catalyst for spiritual growth.   ___ yes   ___ no

Be more compassionate and forgiving toward others.   ___ yes   ___ no

Be willing to make small changes to become what I desire to become.   ___ yes   ___ no

Look beyond surface appearances.   ___ yes   ___ no

Choose to take positive actions instead of dwelling on negative feelings.   ___ yes   ___ no

Put myself in others' shoes.   ___ yes   ___ no

Think the best of others.   ___ yes   ___ no

Things to Do

☐ Pray and ask God to show you what you can learn from your feelings of envy and jealousy.

☐ Do one small thing to cultivate a good quality in your life that you envy in another.

☐ Write a letter to God thanking Him for your blessings, naming them individually.

☐ Write the answer to this question in your journal: How did I get caught up in the envy game?

☐ Have a close friend tell you what she thinks your greatest talents are, then do the same for her.

☐ Do a kindness for someone you envy.

Things to Remember

Whenever you're trying to look better than others or get the better of others, things fall apart and everyone ends up at the others' throats.

JAMES 3:16 THE MESSAGE

Love is patient; love is kind; love is not envious or boastful or arrogant.

1 CORINTHIANS 13:4 NRSV

We're blasted by anger and swamped by rage, but who can survive jealousy?

PROVERBS 27:4 THE MESSAGE

As the elect of God, holy and beloved, put on tender mercies, kindness, humility, meekness, longsuffering.

COLOSSIANS 3:12 NKJV

A man's pride will bring him low, but the humble in spirit will retain honor.

PROVERBS 22:4 NKJV

Whoever desires to become great among you, let him be your servant. And whoever desires to be first among you, let him be your slave.

MATTHEW 20:26–7 NKJV

Don't just pretend to be good! Be done with hypocrisy and jealousy and backstabbing.

1 PETER 2:1 NLT

Envy comes from people's ignorance of, or lack of belief in, their own gifts.

—JEAN VANIER

Envy takes the joy, happiness, and contentment out of living.

—BILLY GRAHAM

Serenity

The Smile of Mary

Return to your rest, O my soul, for the Lord has dealt bountifully with you.

—PSALM 116:7 NKJV

Serenity. You sense it in the old masters' paintings of Mary, with her sweet smile and tranquil expression. You hear it in the music of Mozart and Bach and Brahms, a smooth flow of melody and harmony that soothes your heart and quiets your mind. A beautiful meadow, with sheep grazing and grass as green as a four-leaf clover, is a perfect picture of serenity, as is a tranquil lake mirroring the blue sky. Yet in our frazzled society, serenity is hard to find. You look in the mirror, but instead of a serene smiling face, you see your own worried countenance. Can we achieve serenity in this fast-paced modern age?

The woman who cultivates her relationship to God can discover serenity—a peace that passes understanding. Simplicity, serenity, and tranquility of spirit is possible for the woman who simplifies her life and learns to rest in God.

So often we are frazzled because we have overextended ourselves. We are out of temper because we try to do too much, set unrealistic standards of performance for ourselves and others, try to control and predict every outcome, and generally try to stuff too much into our lives. We then beat ourselves up for not having instant peace and wisdom and wonder why we are so tired, angry, and frustrated. God wants to give us the gift of serenity, peace, and quiet wisdom, if we will only stop long enough to allow Him to do so.

You can find inner serenity no matter what your circumstances, for serenity is tied to your inner trust in God, not to what is going on all around you. Develop serenity in the following ways:

Offer everything to God through an accepting faith, trusting in His ability to provide for and protect you.

Exchange thoughts of worry or anxiety for positive thoughts of faith, affirmation, and hope.

Simplify your life by eliminating the nonessentials and making room for the things of spiritual importance instead.

Believe that all things work together for the highest good.

Do your best in all situations, but don't allow yourself to get too attached to results, thus freeing God to work things out better than you could have planned or imagined.

Engage in quiet prayer and meditation, whether in times you set aside or in the midst of a busy day.

Trust in divine timing and divine wisdom in the midst of uncertain situations.

Choose to cultivate your relationship with God, knowing that He is the source of all true serenity.

I Will

Offer myself to God in faith.   *yes*   *no*

Believe that all things are working together for the
highest good.   *yes*   *no*

Look for ways to simplify my life.   *yes*   *no*

Keep my focus on the most important priorities
instead of allowing myself to become distracted.   *yes*   *no*

Do my best and trust God with the results.   *yes*   *no*

Trust in divine wisdom.   *yes*   *no*

Be faithful instead of fearful.   *yes*   *no*

Things to Do

☐ Set aside regular appointments with God on your personal calendar.

☐ Turn five Bible promises into personal affirmations (example: I trust
   in the Lord with all my heart, Proverbs 3:5).

☐ Keep a record of your daily activities for a week, then look at that
   record in the light of your priorities.

☐ Organize your closets.

☐ Do a thorough spring or fall cleaning of your home.

☐ Practice saying no out loud.

☐ Create a beautiful flower arrangement.

Things to Remember

Thus says the Lord GOD, the Holy One of Israel: "In returning and rest you shall be saved; in quietness and confidence shall be your strength."

ISAIAH 30:15 NKJV

Mary kept all these things and pondered them in her heart.

LUKE 2:19 NKJV

Peace I leave with you, My peace I give to you; not as the world gives do I give to you. Let not your heart be troubled, neither let it be afraid.

JOHN 14:27 NKJV

To be carnally minded is death, but to be spiritually minded is life and peace.

ROMANS 8:6 NKJV

The fruit of righteousness is sown in peace by those who make peace.

JAMES 3:18 NKJV

Blessed are the pure in heart, for they shall see God.

MATTHEW 5:8 KJV

God causes everything to work together for the good of those who love God and are called according to his purpose for them.

ROMANS 8:28 NLT

Grant me the serenity to accept things I cannot change, the courage to change things I can, and the wisdom to know the difference.

—REINHOLD NIEBHUR

Let nothing good or bad upset the balance of your life.

—THOMAS À KEMPIS

Praise

Enjoying God

Praise the LORD! Praise the name of the LORD; praise Him, O you servants of the LORD!

—*PSALM 135:1* NKJV

What an exuberant, joyful command! Praise the Lord! God is worthy to be praised. Not only for what He does, but for who He is. Your praise is a response to the character of God, who He is and what He has done in your life to touch you and to heal you.

We tend to look for God in the phenomenal and grandiose. So when it comes to praising God, we often think of Cecil B. De Mille extravaganzas complete with "Lights! Camera! Action!" We think of an end-times book of Revelation experience with a cast of thousands in full costume, blasting trumpets, and flying flags. Though you are promised in the book of Revelation that you will one day experience a greater scene of praise than any moviemaker can imagine, you can also praise God in the ordinary and common things of life, here and now.

Everyday praise includes singing songs to God as you do dishes or vacuum the floor. You can praise God when you put on your makeup—look in the mirror and thank

Him for the face you were born with, the face you are putting on for the world, and the face that reflects a loving heart no matter what your outward style may be. You can praise Him every day with a grace before meals. Offer thanksgiving for the small blessings you enjoy—from the cup of coffee you drink to the sheets and blankets that keep you warm at night. Did your car start this morning? Praise God. Did your car need to be towed to a mechanic for repair instead? Praise God anyway, especially if you have an honest mechanic who will fix your car for a fair price. Praise God on the freeway or in the school parking lot. Praise God in the grocery store or at the churchwomen's committee meeting. Praise Him for the child's sticky kiss or the husband's morning hug or the phone call from a friend. In everything give thanks. Praise the Lord!

The whole Bible is punctuated with outbursts of praise. It comes spontaneously from the joy that characterizes God's people. Does the joy of the Lord characterize you? Do you take pleasure and delight in God's creation—and remember to share that pleasure with God? When you praise Him, you participate in the coming of God's kingdom to earth, even if only in a small acknowledgment that He is your Lord and worthy of your praise.

I Will

Praise God with all my heart.   _yes_   _no_

Be alert to small blessings in my day.   _yes_   _no_

Have a thankful heart.   _yes_   _no_

Avoid complaining.   _yes_   _no_

Be aware of opportunities to praise God in
the midst of my day.   _yes_   _no_

Joyfully sing songs of praise to God.   _yes_   _no_

Take delight in being God's child.   _yes_   _no_

Things to Do

☐ Write your own personal prayer of praise and say it to God.

☐ Memorize a psalm of praise (perhaps Psalm 117).

☐ Number a page from 1 to 100. Write down 100 things you praise God
for in your life.

☐ Join with other believers in praise and worship this Sunday.

☐ Write a letter to someone you admire, in appreciation for his or her
contribution to your life.

☐ Sing a song of praise to God the next time you do the dishes or other
household chore alone.

☐ Do a topical Bible study on praise.

Things to Remember

Holy, holy, holy, Lord God Almighty,
who was and is and is to come!

REVELATION 4:8 NKJV

We all, with unveiled face, beholding as
in a mirror the glory of the Lord, are
being transformed into the same image
from glory to glory, just as by the Spirit
of the Lord.

2 CORINTHIANS 3:18 NKJV

Mary said: "My soul magnifies the Lord,
and my spirit has rejoiced in God my
Savior."

LUKE 1:46–47 NKJV

Let us continually offer the sacrifice of
praise to God, that is, the fruit of our
lips, giving thanks to His name.

HEBREWS 13:15 NKJV

Be glad and rejoice forever in what I
create; for behold, I create Jerusalem as a
rejoicing, and her people a joy.

ISAIAH 65:18 NKJV

I will praise the name of God with a
song, and will magnify Him with
thanksgiving.

PSALM 69:30 NKJV

*Praise not merely
expresses but
completes the
enjoyment; it is its
appointed
consummation. . . .
In commending us
to glorify Him, God
is inviting us to
enjoy Him.*

—C. S. LEWIS

*You don't learn to
praise in a day,
especially since you
may have been
complaining for
years! New habits
take time to develop.
But you can begin
today, and practice
tomorrow, and the
next day, until it
becomes a part
of you.*

—ERWIN W. LUTZER

Letting Go

Holding Life with an Open Hand

My soul, wait silently for God alone, for my expectation is from Him.

—*PSALM* 62:5 NKJV

Place a small rock in the open palm of your hand. Now clench your fist around that rock, holding it tightly, keeping your muscles rigid and tense. How long can you hold this position comfortably? Notice how quickly your hand tires. Now open your hand again, allowing the rock to lie comfortably in the center of your open palm. Do you think you could hold the rock more comfortably for a longer period of time in this open position?

Our bodies illustrate spiritual lessons. How often have you clutched your life in a clenched fist, fighting the natural forces, trying to control and confine life within the small boundaries of your fears and expectations? It is as uncomfortable for the human heart to be clenched and closed as it is for the human hand. We were meant for openness, movement, and freedom.

The apostle Paul had to learn a new way of relating to

life after he encountered the risen Christ on the road to Damascus. He spent fourteen years in obscurity learning the lessons that would free him to fulfill his highest calling. He had to overcome a negative law-oriented religion to discover that freedom in Christ is the goal of the law he had been taught. He had to let go all the legalism of his upbringing, filtering out the negative use of doctrine that taught judgment and argument, replacing them with the fruit of the Spirit— gentleness, patience, love. He learned to allow God to lead him down roads he had never dreamed of taking, discovering the freedom of grace in the process.

So it is with you. You may be dealing with harsh expectation of yourself, frustration with circumstances you have tried too long to control, or disappointment because things didn't happen the way you thought they should. The harder you try to conform life to your preconceived patterns, the more frustrated and angry you become. Only by letting go and letting God can you ever find the joy and freedom you so anxiously seek.

Grace is a gift that God gives to an open hand. If your hand is closed, you have no room to receive the surprise packages of life and love that God offers. Unclench your fist. Instead of trying to second-guess, judge, and control life, allow God to surprise you with new insight and unexpected gifts. Let go your rigid opinions and limited expectations. Open your heart and hand to receive God's gifts of grace and freedom and delight.

I Will

Let go and let God.   _yes_   _no_

Allow God to surprise me.   _yes_   _no_

Have a teachable heart.   _yes_   _no_

Let go of unrealistic expectations.   _yes_   _no_

Be flexible instead of rigid.   _yes_   _no_

Live in grace by faith.   _yes_   _no_

Embrace a new freedom in my life.   _yes_   _no_

Things to Do

☐ Reflect on Galatians 6:15 and think about the times God did something new in your life.

☐ Take a different route to work tomorrow.

☐ Do a topical Bible study on the Pharisees.

☐ Go to the library and check out a book on a subject you've never read about before.

☐ Try a new restaurant for a change.

☐ Get together with a group of friends to brainstorm exciting new ideas.

☐ Plant a new kind of seed in your garden this year.

Things to Remember

Obsession with self in these matters is a dead end; attention to God leads us out into the open, into a spacious free life.

ROMANS 8:6 THE MESSAGE

When it pleased God, who separated me from my mother's womb and called me through His grace, to reveal His Son in me, that I might preach among the Gentiles, I did not immediately confer with flesh and blood.

GALATIANS 1:15–16 NKJV

Paul, a bondservant of Jesus Christ, called to be an apostle, separated to the gospel of God, which He promised before through His prophets in the Holy Scriptures.

ROMANS 1:1 NKJV

Can't you see the central issue in all this? It is not what you and I do. It is what God is doing, and he is creating something totally new, a free life!

GALATIANS 6:15 THE MESSAGE

Trust in the LORD forever, for the LORD, the LORD, is the Rock eternal.

ISAIAH 26:4 NIV

Live carefree before God; he is most careful with you.

1 PETER 5:7 THE MESSAGE

God forces no one, for love cannot compel, and God's service, therefore, is a thing of perfect freedom.

—HANS DENCK

The Spirit of God first imparts love; he next inspires hope, and then gives liberty; and that is about the last thing we have in many of our churches.

—D. L. MOODY

Everyday Miracles

Take a Look Around

---

*Whoever is wise will observe these things, and they will
understand the lovingkindness of the LORD.*

—PSALM 107:43 NKJV

Remember when you were a child, how everything seemed
so new and delightful? Remember getting up in the morning,
knowing that you were going to explore a big wonderful world
full of mysteries and sensations and surprises? Have you as an
adult forgotten the miracle of material things, taking the gifts
of this life for granted? If so, it's time for a refresher course in
appreciating God's creation, human ingenuity, and everyday
miracles.

Start with the morning. When was the last time you "woke
up and smelled the coffee"? If you've been to a gourmet coffee
shop lately, you know that coffee isn't just coffee any more. It
might have been ground coffee from a vacuum-packed can in
your mother's day, but now getting a simple cup of joe can be
a major life decision. Here are a few choices from a local
specialty foods shop: Sumatra Mandehling, Tanzania Peaberry,
Kenya Estate Java, Ethiopian Yergachefee, Mexican Organic,
and Classic French Roast. Each type represents a country, a

culture, and a lifestyle. Imagine the coffee beans growing in the sun and rain, the hands that picked them, the people who packaged and shipped them across the miles to you. Think about how many people had to work together to bring you a "simple" cup of coffee. And that's before you've ordered your espresso drink! (Make that a grande café mocha Americana with whipped cream, please.)

But the morning's miracles are only beginning. Who designed the pattern on your china plate and your coffee cup? Whose creativity contributed to the refrigerator that cooled your orange juice, the stove where you cooked your eggs, and the table where you ate your breakfast? Blessings and miracles galore—and it isn't even nine o'clock yet. And, by the way, where did you get such an interesting clock to decorate the wall over your kitchen table?

Look out the window. You may see the flash of red cardinal wing, hear the defiant scream of a boisterous blue jay, or catch the chirp of a chickadee hiding in the forsythia bush. While you've been inside the world outside has been on its own errands. Ants and earthworms and birds and bees have all been about their business. Even in the dead of winter, nature is doing its own thing outside your door. Another endless source of miracles to marvel at!

After breakfast, it's time to look into your closet and choose something to wear. More small miracles. The dress that doesn't fit may remind you of the five pounds you'd like to lose. But that lovely angora sweater is so soft, and the suit you plan to wear to work is not only flattering, it makes you feel like a million bucks.

Step outside your door. Whatever the weather is outside, you can be sure there's plenty of it. Rain or shine, sultry or snowy, sunny or cloudy, you know that the weather will be changing sooner or later. Weather and seasons demonstrate that God likes variety. You may grizzle about the drizzle, but a sunny blue spring sky is guaranteed to make any spirit soar.

And so it goes. Every day you encounter miracles. Every day God is giving you gifts, showering you with abundance. And every day it's your choice whether you are going to take them for granted, complain that there aren't enough, or be thankful that you are so blessed.

Awareness and gratitude go hand in hand. Jesus said that those with childlike hearts would see the kingdom of God. If you look at your own seemingly mundane life through the eyes of a child, you'll begin to see that you are surrounded by miracles. As you learn to cultivate awareness of the small things in life, and to value them, you'll also begin to understand God's constant love and care for you. He designed this wonderful creation. Yes, pain and sin and sorrow exist. Creation may be fallen with mosquitoes and ticks along with fireflies and stars. But even with all its faults, it is a beautiful creation that reflects the creativity if its Creator. And maybe, just maybe, the next time you look in the mirror, you'll also realize that you, too, are one of God's miracles. You can count on it, every single day.

No matter what happens, always be thankful.

—1 Thessalonians 5:18 NLT

I Will

Cultivate a childlike heart.   _yes_   _no_

Be aware of small things.   _yes_   _no_

See material things as small miracles from
the hand of God.   _yes_   _no_

Be grateful for the blessings of daily life.   _yes_   _no_

Enjoy ordinary life more.   _yes_   _no_

Appreciate the work of all the people who contribute
to the functioning of my daily life.   _yes_   _no_

Look for signs of the kingdom of heaven in the
mundane things of earth.   _yes_   _no_

Things to Do

☐ Make a list of a hundred ordinary things and praise God for each one
of them.

☐ Take a walk in your neighborhood.

☐ Go to a coffee or tea shop and learn about all the different varieties
and the countries they come from.

☐ Pray for your plumber, sanitation worker, mail carrier, mechanic,
grocery checkout clerk, and server at the coffee shop.

☐ Leave an extra large tip for your server as an unseen thank offering to
God.

☐ Go barefoot and feel the earth between your toes.

Things to Remember

He has made His wonderful works to be remembered; the LORD is gracious and full of compassion.

PSALM 111:4 NKJV

Offer to God a sacrifice of thanksgiving and pay your vows to the Most High.

PSALM 50:14 NRSV

I applied my heart to know, to search and seek out wisdom and the reason for things.

ECCLESIASTES 7:25 NKJV

From the rising of the sun to its going down, the LORD's name is to be praised.
—PSALM 113:3 NKJV

Be joyful always: pray continuously; give thanks in all circumstances, for this is God's will for you in Christ Jesus.

1 THESSALONIANS 5:16–18 NIV

Thanks be to God for his indescribable gift!

2 CORINTHIANS 9:15 NRSV

A pretentious showy life is an empty life; a plain and simple life is a full life.

PROVERBS 13:7 THE MESSAGE

The righteous eats to the satisfying of his soul, but the stomach of the wicked shall be in want.

PROVERBS 13:25 NKJV

Truly the light is sweet, and it is pleasant for the eyes to behold the sun.

ECCLESIASTES 11:7 NKJV

Therefore my heart is glad, and my glory rejoices; my flesh also will rest in hope.

PSALM 16:9 NKJV

If you are happy, sing psalms.

JAMES 5:13 GOD'S WORD

Let the peace that comes from Christ rule in your hearts. For as members of one body you are all called to live in peace. And always be thankful.

COLOSSIANS 3:15 NLT

Since evertything God created is good, we should not reject any of it. We may receive it gladly, with thankful hearts.

1 TIMOTHY 4:4 NLT

Gratitude to God makes even a temporal blessing a taste of heaven.

—WILLIAM ROMAINE

In ordinary life we hardly realize that we receive a great more than we give, and that it is only with gratitude that life becomes rich.

—DIETRICH BONHOEFFER

Optimism

You Find What You Look For

He who earnestly seeks good finds favor, but trouble will come to him who seeks evil.

—*PROVERBS 11:27* NKJV

Life has its ups and downs. We love the up times, but oh, how we hate the down times. After many disappointments and difficult times, it's sometimes hard to believe for the best. We become cynical and jaded, ashamed to be vulnerable and childlike, afraid that our hopes and dreams are foolish in the "real world" that often seems to reward cold calculation. Yet when we close our hearts to optimism and faith, we close the door on making our dreams come true in this world. By choosing an optimistic attitude, however, we open ourselves to the possibility that God can turn our negative situations into something positive.

You can choose to be optimistic. Optimism is a learned attitude of faith. Faith is a choice, not an argument. It is an inner conviction, an unshakable assurance. You make a decision to choose optimism, choosing to believe that God will truly work all things together for good.

Focusing on the negatives in any situation is counterproductive. You concentrate on what's wrong, and soon that's the only thing you can see. Here are some of the negative thoughts that hold us back: *I can't. I won't. That's a problem. It's not fair. It won't work. Stupid. Impossible. Hopeless. It's too hard. I'm not good enough. What a drag. But we never did it that way before.*

Positive thoughts help us make positive choices. Choose to replace negative patterns with positive, empowering thoughts like these: *I can. It's possible. I'll give it a try. Let's go. Yes. I will. It will work. I am able to do this. It will be fun.*

Learn to look for the silver lining in the dark clouds of your life. Expect God to bring you good or to bring good out of a bad situation. Focus on the positives. See the glass as half-full instead of as half-empty. Wash the windows of your soul by asking God to cleanse your thoughts every day, replacing negative defeatist thoughts with positive affirmations of faith and hope.

The book of Hebrews talks about running the race, leaving behind those things that would encumber you and drag you down. Let go of those negative thoughts, and train yourself to focus on a positive outcome instead of looking for potential disaster. Learn to see that every stumbling block can be a stepping-stone. You will find what you look for, see what you want to see. If you want to reach the goal of a life well lived, learn to look with optimism and faith.

I Will

Have faith in God.   _yes_   _no_

Expect God to bring good even in negative
situations.   _yes_   _no_

See every stumbling block as a stepping-stone.   _yes_   _no_

Be optimistic about outcomes.   _yes_   _no_

Choose a positive attitude.   _yes_   _no_

Focus on the positive instead of the negative.   _yes_   _no_

Be open to new possibilities.   _yes_   _no_

Things to Do

☐ In your journal write about an unexpected blessing that came at a
difficult time in your life.

☐ For just one day, replace every negative word or comment with a
positive word or comment.

☐ Make a personal affirmation from a Bible verse (perhaps Psalm
118:24) and say it first thing every morning for the next week.

☐ Develop a friendship with someone new.

☐ Write your worries in the sand at the beach.

☐ Plant a flower or vegetable garden.

☐ List ten "impossible" things you would like to do or try. Do one.

Things to Remember

This is the day the LORD has made, we will rejoice and be glad in it.

PSALM 118:24 NKJV

Since we are surrounded by so great a cloud of witnesses, let us lay aside every weight, and the sin which so easily ensnares us, and let us run with endurance the race that is set before us.

HEBREWS 12:1 NKJV

Optimism is the faith that leads to achievement. Nothing can be done without hope and confidence.

—HELEN KELLER

Therefore, having been justified by faith, we have peace with God through our Lord Jesus Christ, through whom also we have access by faith into this grace in which we stand, and rejoice in hope of the glory of God.

ROMANS 5:1–2 NKJV

As you travel on through life, whatever be your goal, keep your eye on the doughnut and not upon the hole.

—AUTHOR UNKNOWN

Therefore do not cast away your confidence, which has great reward.

HEBREWS 10:35 NKJV

Let us hold fast the confession of our hope without wavering, for He who promised is faithful.

HEBREWS 10:23 NKJV

Your eyes are windows into your body. If you open your eyes wide in wonder and belief, your body fills up with light.

MATTHEW 6:22 THE MESSAGE

Gifts

The Present

There are diversities of gifts, but the same Spirit.

—*1 Corinthians 12:4* NKJV

There are many gifts that come from God. We are given the gift of life, our very existence on this earth. The beautiful and diverse creation that surrounds us is a present wrapped in wonder and wildness. Our individual circumstances, our creative talents, and our unique personalities are all gifts from the hand of God. There is the gift of salvation that is offered freely through Jesus Christ and the gift of the written word of God that speaks straight to our hearts. God offers spiritual gifts for those who seek them, as well.

You received special gifts as a woman. Your femininity, your ability to bear and nurture children, your creativity and homemaking skills, and your gentle tenderness are some of the gifts of being a woman. As a woman you can express the gift of your personality and style in many ways. You may like florals and lace or sleek modern lines. You may be soft and voluptuous, lean and athletic, or wiry and strong. No matter what kind of package you come in, you offer the gift of a feminine viewpoint that balances a masculine way of looking at the world.

Some gifts come wrapped in attractive packages, like talent or beauty or ability. But God's gifts can sometimes come wrapped in unattractive packages. You may wish you were taller, thinner, more beautiful; or that you had been raised in a different kind of family or had another, better version of your own life. But accepting the entire package, instead of just the parts you like, is a lesson in life you have to learn.

Do you appreciate the gifts that God has given you? Your gift to God is accepting and using the gifts He gave you. You show your appreciation of your God-given gifts by learning about them and understanding that they are His good plan for you. Then you develop them to the best of your ability. As you use your gifts and serve others, you can enter into a new joy and discover the fullness of God's plans for your life.

Each moment is a gift if you have the eyes to see and the heart to appreciate it. The perfect gift is the present, the here and now. The past is history and the future is a mystery. You do not know what will happen tomorrow and you cannot change what happened in the past, but this moment offers the gift of choosing what you will do right now. Will you accept the present with gratitude and appreciation?

I Will

Thank God for the gifts He has given me. _yes_ _no_

Accept the opportunities and limitations of my life
as gifts from God. _yes_ _no_

Cultivate my natural abilities. _yes_ _no_

Serve others with love. _yes_ _no_

Be grateful for the gifts each moment brings. _yes_ _no_

Enjoy the gift of femininity. _yes_ _no_

Be open to accepting even the unattractive and
difficult gifts of life. _yes_ _no_

Things to Do

☐ Do a topical Bible study on spiritual gifts.

☐ Give an extra 10 percent over your usual giving for the next three
months.

☐ Create a theme gift basket (bath and body, Italian dinner, garden) and
give it to someone.

☐ List twenty-five gifts that God gave you today (such as spring flowers, a
car that starts, a kiss).

☐ Go to a nursing home and spend an afternoon offering the gift of your
time and a listening ear.

☐ Take a class to learn a new skill or to develop an old skill.

Things to Remember

If you then, being evil, know how to give good gifts to your children, how much more will your Father who is in heaven give good things to those who ask Him!

MATTHEW 7:11 NKJV

A present is a precious stone in the eyes of its possessor; wherever he turns, he prospers.

PROVERBS 17:8 NKJV

Every good and perfect gift comes down from the Father who created all the lights in the heavens.

JAMES 2:17 CEV

Having then gifts differing according to the grace that is given to us, let us use them.

ROMANS 12:6 NKJV

The gifts and the calling of God are irrevocable.

ROMANS 11:29 NKJV

Jesus answered and said to her, "If you knew the gift of God, and who it is who says to you, 'Give me a drink,' you would have asked Him, and He would have given you living water."

JOHN 4:10 NKJV

Be ready at all times for the gifts of God, and always for new ones.

—MEISTER ECKHART

God's gifts put man's best dreams to shame.

—ELISABETH BARRETT BROWNING

Openness

Holy Curiosity

Jesus said, "Your eyes are windows into your body. If you open your eyes wide in wonder and belief, your body fills up with light."

—MATTHEW 6:22 THE MESSAGE

Did you ever think of curiosity as holy? In school, you may have been told to be curious, but were then rewarded for obedience and for rote recital of the answers. You learned quickly that you shouldn't ask too many questions. As an adolescent, conformity was extremely important. You didn't want to be too different or to expose your vulnerabilities. In your school it may have been considered geeky to be too smart or too interested in your lessons. As an adult, the corporation may give lip service to creativity, but you may often observe that conformity is what is rewarded. Even in church, you may be encouraged not to rock the boat. It is easy to forget that when the Spirit enters the heart, a revolution comes and transformation occurs.

Holy curiosity is a way of exploring the world with childlike wonder, eyes wide open to see what others miss. Jesus said to be like a child to enter the kingdom of heaven. He emphasized that the heart should be open and tender, ready for God to teach new lessons. Jesus also taught people to look at the common things around them with different eyes. Seed and sower, housewives and vineyard keepers, birds and flowers—His parables showed the world through another lens, turning the things people took for granted into living pictures of the kingdom of God.

You can choose to be open to God doing something new and surprising in your life—and in the lives of other people. Delight in being more open toward others. Instead of saying "he always does" or "she never will," ask instead how you can have compassion and understanding for those who are difficult to deal with. Talk to someone who has a different opinion or belief and really, really listen. Look for fresh ways of cultivating new and old relationships instead of expecting that things will be the same as they have always been.

Be an explorer. Experiment and go on mental, spiritual, and physical adventures. Openness and acceptance free you from being too judgmental and set in your ways. Instead of assuming that you understand how things should be and how they should work out, let your struggles and limitations and questions become an open door to unexpected opportunities and knowledge. Be willing to experiment, to ask questions, to look at the familiar in unfamiliar ways. Lighten up and be playful, like a child. Say yes to new adventures instead of no. Cultivate an open mind and heart—and claim your freedom in Christ.

I Will

Enjoy the vastness and variety of God's creation. *yes* *no*

Be open to the unexpected. *yes* *no*

Cultivate curiosity. *yes* *no*

Seek out new experiences and new people. *yes* *no*

Keep an open mind. *yes* *no*

Be playful in my explorations. *yes* *no*

Be willing to be a beginner and make mistakes. *yes* *no*

Things to Do

☐ Listen to a missionary share his or her adventures or join a short mission trip.

☐ Go to an outdoor lecture or take a guided hike at a state or national park.

☐ Chaperone a group of young people on a retreat or field trip.

☐ Try a new color of lipstick.

☐ Visit a museum of natural history or an aquarium or zoo.

☐ Go to the library and check out an interesting book on a subject you know nothing about.

☐ Try a new kind of exercise—if you walk, learn to swim; if you run, try biking.

Things to Remember

If the Son sets you free, you are free
through and through.

JOHN 8:36 THE MESSAGE

Behold, I do a new thing, now it shall
spring forth; shall you not know it? I
will even make a road in the wilderness
and rivers in the desert.

ISAIAH 43:19 NKJV

A man who isolates himself seeks his
own desire; he rages against all wise
judgment.

PROVERBS 18:1 NKJV

Happy is the man who finds wisdom,
and the man who gains understanding.

PROVERBS 3:13 NKJV

Christ has set us free to live a free life.
So take your stand! Never again let
anyone put a harness of slavery on you.

GALATIANS 5:1 THE MESSAGE

One thing I have desired of the LORD,
that will I seek, that I may dwell in the
house of the LORD all the days of my life,
to behold the beauty of the LORD, and to
inquire in His temple.

PSALM 27:4 NKJV

*Always be in a state
of expectancy and see
that you leave room
for God to come in
as He likes.*

—OSWALD CHAMBERS

*If we knew what we
were doing, it
wouldn't be called
"research," would it?*

—ALBERT EINSTEIN

Heaven

A Glimpse of Glory

In My Father's house are many mansions; if it were not so, I would have told you. I go to prepare a place for you.

—JOHN 14:2 NKJV

This life is not all that there is. As a believer, heaven is your hope. Precious promises in the Bible remind you that God has a greater plan and that your life does not end with death, but begins anew beyond the grave in the presence of God. Jesus promises that He will prepare an eternal place that is beyond sorrow, tears, loss, suffering, and death.

Heaven can also be tasted in earthly things. A child's eyes, a snowdrop blossom pushing through the snow, young lambs frolicking in a green field, and the dewy newness of spring are reminders of resurrection promises and heavenly bliss. Church bells in the distance, beautiful symphonies, angelic choirs, and glorious voices offer reminders of the heavenly music that will be made in the City of God. Paintings of angels and saints by the old masters tell the story of God's plan of redemption and the fulfillment of a new heaven and earth, when He will wipe away all tears.

Though a secular society might discount these pictures of heaven as fantasy and myth, Christians believe that they are part of a greater, higher reality than mere materialism can comprehend. Christians believe that God not only made creation, but is intimately involved in His creation and has a happy ending in store. Christians died in Roman arenas because they believed in a kingdom where Jesus Christ reigns forever in beauty, majesty, justice, and love.

In the Lord's Prayer, you ask that God's will be done on earth as it is in heaven. You can bring the kingdom of heaven to earth in your heart and in your life by your attitude, acts of kindness and love, and willingness to worship God in beauty, simplicity, and holiness.

Here are a few suggestions for making a little heaven on earth today.

Pamper your loved ones today. Make a special meal. Grant a longed-for wish. Cuddle and hug them, and whisper words of love in their ears. Your husband, your children, your parents—all whom you love—need to be reminded in practical ways that you care.

Wear a beautiful dress, make home a haven, and create beauty and order where you can. Beauty is a blessing that speaks of heaven without words.

Take a long walk in God's creation and savor the earthly beauties that remind you of God's love and creativity.

Light a candle and worship God in the beauty and silence of prayer.

I Will

Live my life as if my choices had eternal value and
eternal consequences. _____yes_____ _____no_____

Trust that God has a place prepared for me in heaven. _____yes_____ _____no_____

Look for heaven's beauties on earth. _____yes_____ _____no_____

Know that I understand in part and will know in full
in eternity. _____yes_____ _____no_____

Try my best to create a little bit of heaven on earth
wherever I am. _____yes_____ _____no_____

Create beauty and order in my life. _____yes_____ _____no_____

Worship God in the beauty of holiness. _____yes_____ _____no_____

Things to Do

☐ Spend an hour talking with children about heaven.

☐ Read 1 Corinthians 15:35–58.

☐ Buy a CD of music that inspires and uplifts you.

☐ Visit a famous cathedral and see heaven visualized in stone
and stained glass and light.

☐ Walk in a forest and see glimpses of heaven on earth.

☐ Do a New Testament study on heaven.

☐ Grow a fragrant blooming plant on your winter windowsill.

Things to Remember

Jesus said, "Do not fear little flock, for it is your Father's good pleasure to give you the kingdom."

LUKE 12:13 NKJV

Surely goodness and mercy shall follow me all the days of my life; and I will dwell in the house of the LORD forever.

PSALM 23:6 NKJV

When it's sin versus grace, grace wins hands down. All sin can do is threaten us with death, and that's the end of it. Grace, because God is putting everything together again through the Messiah, invites us into life—a life that goes on and on and on, world without end.

ROMANS 5:10–21 THE MESSAGE

I saw a new heaven and new earth. The first heaven and the first earth had disappeared, and so had the sea.

REVELATION 2:1 CEV

Jesus said, "I am the living bread which came down from heaven. If anyone eats of this bread, he will live forever; and the bread that I shall give is My flesh, which I shall give for the life of the world."

JOHN 6:51 NKJV

Joy is the serious business of heaven.

—C. S. LEWIS

If you are a Christian, you are not a citizen of this world trying to get to heaven; you are a citizen of heaven making your way through this world.

—VANCE HAVNER

Contentment

The Glass Is Half Full

Bless the Lord, O my soul, and forget not all His benefits.
—*PSALM 103:2* NKJV

Do you see the glass as half full—or half empty? A contented person knows that the glass is half full, of course. Contentment is not the same as happiness. Happiness depends on circumstances—wishes granted, goals achieved, gifts given, and things going our way. Contentment takes the more common path, focusing on what you already have instead of trying to get what you want.

Contentment is a matter of attitude. Contented attitudes come from appreciating the small, commonplace things of life—things that you may often take for granted. Even the most sorrowful life has moments of contentment. You may or may not have happy circumstances, but you have the choice to be constantly contented or constantly dissatisfied with your life.

A child already knows the art of being contented. Walking along the trail beside Daddy and Mommy, she stops to pick up an acorn. She loves the smooth feel of the nut in her hand, fingering its rough top. She learns from Daddy that squirrels love nuts and sees the flash of gray fur as two squirrels chase each other up a tree. An ice-cream cone presents a total sensuous experience, to be tasted with eyes and fingers and nose as well as tongue. A soft velvet dress is stroked like a kitten's fur. Yet on a rainy day, a mud puddle is irresistible for splashing and stomping. The squishy feel of mud between the fingers is as fascinating as the most complex and elegant gift to a child. How many times have you seen a child unwrap dozens of Christmas presents only to find her playing later with the box it came in? For a child, everything is a source of wonder and delight.

Cultivate contentment by living in the present. Enjoy the everyday gifts with a child's sense of wonder. Savor the scents and smells and sounds and textures of your life. When you make scrambled eggs in the morning, really taste their eggy richness. Stop and smell the coffee. Breathe in the scent of a rose. Listen to the sigh of the wind, the chatter of morning birdsong.

Find contentment in the small rituals of every day. Drinking a cup of tea. Having a quiet time every morning with prayer and Bible reading. Enjoy the sensation of the car moving smoothly down the highway as you commute to work or run errands. Be thankful for the kiss at night when you greet your husband at the door.

Make time for leisured contentment. Enjoy the feel of earth in your hands as you plant and cultivate a garden. Read a good book by a winter hearthside. Go for a long walk or drive or bicycle ride down a country road, and admire haystacks and cows and trees and wildflowers that grow in abundance in the ditch by the side of the road. Stop for a few minutes to admire a gorgeous sunset.

Cultivate your relationships. There is contentment aplenty in a cozy conversation over a cup of steaming tea. Hold hands with your husband and enjoy kissing his cheek after he's just shaved. Cuddle with your kids and teach them the games you loved to play in childhood. Make time for family fun. Schedule meetings with friends who share your interests and encourage each other on life's journey. Give time to causes you believe in and create community by doing good together.

Celebrate beauty and goodness wherever you find it. An awareness of life's beauty enriches the spirit, reminding you that life is not all about drudgery, traffic, bills, and lists of things to do. Buy a single rose or a cheery bouquet to brighten your day. Buy an extra one to share with someone else. Don't let clothes sit in the closet, waiting for the special occasion that never comes. Wear a favorite dress or outfit and make today a special occasion, just because. Make your home as lovely as possible, tastefully arranging the things you treasure. Enjoy a simple collection of stones or seashells or fall leaves that remind you of nature's bounty.

Cultivating a contented attitude of gratitude and appreciation can help you cope with difficult situations and develop the ability to see silver linings in dark clouds and rainbows in the rain. Choose contentment and reap its gentle rewards.

He has satisfied the hungry with good things.

—Luke 1:53 NLT

I Will

Praise God for the gifts He gives each day.   *yes*   *no*

Cultivate a contented attitude.   *yes*   *no*

Find delight in the small things in life.   *yes*   *no*

Live in the moment instead of worrying about
tomorrow.   *yes*   *no*

Look for ways to share good things with others.   *yes*   *no*

Commit to spending more time with those I love.   *yes*   *no*

Celebrate goodness.   *yes*   *no*

Things to Do

- [ ] List fifty blessings you enjoyed today.

- [ ] Write in your journal your thoughts about why your glass is half full instead of half empty.

- [ ] Make a pot of soup and share it.

- [ ] Learn how to do a simple home craft such as quilting or knitting that can be a soothing and repetitive everyday ritual.

- [ ] Get together with friends for tea and talk.

- [ ] Pick a favorite novel and reread it.

- [ ] Spend an afternoon in front of a cozy fire.

Things to Remember

Actually, I don't have a sense of needing anything personally. I've learned by now to be quite content whatever my circumstances. I'm just as happy with little as with much, with much as with little.

PHILIPPIANS 4:11 THE MESSAGE

I know that nothing is better for them than to rejoice, and to do good in their lives, and also that every man should eat and drink and enjoy the good of all his labor—it is the gift of God.

ECCLESIASTES 3:12–13 NKJV

Better is a little with the fear of the LORD, than great treasure with trouble.
—PROVERBS 15:16 NKJV

I've found the recipe for being happy whether full or hungry, hands full or hands empty. Whatever I have, wherever I am, I can make it through anything in the One who makes me who I am.

PHILIPPIANS 4:12–13 THE MESSAGE

A faithful man will abound with blessings, but he who hastens to be rich will not go unpunished.

PROVERBS 28:20 NKJV

You, LORD, have made me glad through Your work; I will triumph in the works of Your hands.

PSALM 92:4 NKJV

I will sing of the mercies of the LORD forever; with my mouth will I make known Your faithfulness to all generations.

PSALM 89:1 NKJV

There is one who makes himself rich, yet has nothing; and one who makes himself poor, yet has great riches.

PROVERBS 13:7 NKJV

There is great gain in godliness combined with contentment; for we brought nothing into the world, so that we can take nothing out of it; but if we have food and clothing, we will be content with these.

1 TIMOTHY 6:6–8 NRSV

Be content with such things as ye have: for he hath said, I will never leave thee nor forsake thee.

HEBREWS 13:5 KJV

I have kept my soul calm and quiet. My soul is content.

PSALM 131:2 NLT

He who is not contented with little will never be satisfied with much.

—THOMAS BENTON BROOKS

Life is a great bundle of little things.

—OLIVER WENDELL HOLMES

Community

Social Graces

If God so loved us, we also ought to love one another.

—1 JOHN 4:11 NKJV

What is community? Community is a supportive environment where we meet together, share common resources, work to achieve common goals, and enjoy a diversity of people who enrich our lives. Rooted in the word *communion*, community is an old-fashioned concept that is being revitalized by those who are disenchanted with a lonely, individualistic society and who want to celebrate the social grace of community once more.

In a modern world, where everything is a commodity to be bought and sold, sharing resources and creating community can sound like a utopian dream. Yet it wasn't very far back in history that community was the means of survival, bringing people together to supply the necessities of life. Comparing a small town with its web of reciprocal relationships to the fortress-mentality of today's gated communities shows how the meaning of real community has changed.

You don't have to live in a small town or idyllic world to create community. You have the raw materials all around you. You create a community by paying attention to the grace inherent in your situation, by becoming aware of those around you and by learning how you can help them connect with one another.

First of all, you have a community of family and friends. These may be scattered across the country, but you still keep in touch and celebrate the meaningful moments of life together. It's important to call your mom and wish her happy birthday, to giggle with a gaggle of girlfriends at a wedding shower, and to cry with loved ones at a funeral. These are the people with whom you share Thanksgiving dinners and Christmas parties and Fourth of July picnics. For many people, their church community also functions as a family, filling the spaces left empty by those who are gone or separated.

Work creates its own form of community. Colleagues often enrich your life with shared goals and common interests. Neighborhoods can be communities where you meet and mingle with people who may lead very different lives but who live on the same street. You may also feel connected to the greater communities of city, state, and country. In times of crisis, communities can be created spontaneously to meet a need or address a trouble. Even a football game can create a temporary community, as you cheer for the home team to win.

Community meets your social needs. Community also stretches your faith and challenges you to become mature. You learn to think about the needs of others. You also look for creative ways to express God's love for them. Some simple ways you can practice the social grace of creating community include:

Speak to people instead of ignoring or rushing past them. Enjoy a little spontaneous conversation. You never know what you'll learn from another person.

Learn people's names and remember to call them by name when you see them. People feel valued and important when you remember who they are.

Smile. There is nothing like a smile to reach across the barriers that separate one stranger from another.

Be friendly and helpful. Open doors, offer to carry something when you see someone is burdened, give a cheery word of encouragement to those who cross your path today.

Be genuinely interested in people. Every person has a unique story. There are everyday heroes to be discovered wherever you look.

Be considerate of the feelings of others. Watch that you don't step on someone's emotional toes without realizing it.

Be thoughtful of the opinions of others. Even if you think someone is wrong, you need to be sensitive to his or her beliefs and feelings.

Be generous with praise and cautious with criticism. People blossom under the warm sun of appreciation and wither in the heat of judgment.

Be willing to serve others. Christ calls you to be a servant, and to care for others.

These are simple social graces that help make genuine community possible. When you are patient, supportive, encouraging, open, and kind, you become a center around which community happens. You don't have to do anything fancy. Just make yourself available to love and appreciate people. When you do, you'll discover that you're part of a warm, supportive community.

I Will

Look for ways to create community in my life.   *yes*   *no*

Be friendly and helpful.   *yes*   *no*

Be considerate of others' feelings.   *yes*   *no*

Be generous with praise and cautious with criticism.   *yes*   *no*

Serve others in love.   *yes*   *no*

Respect our differences and seek to find common
interests.   *yes*   *no*

Enjoy the people God has brought into my life.   *yes*   *no*

Things to Do

☐ Invite a newcomer to your Bible study group.

☐ Host a party or get-together at your house.

☐ Participate in a volleyball game or other group activity.

☐ Make a donation to a charity.

☐ When you are feeling low, send flowers, make a call, or reach out
and help someone else.

☐ Make a collage of pictures of family and friends.

☐ Volunteer to help build a Habitat for Humanity house in your
community.

Things to Remember

A new commandment I give to you, that you love one another; as I have loved you, that you also love one another. By this all will know that you are My disciples, if you have love for one another.

JOHN 13:34–35 NKJV

If someone says, "I love God," and hates his brother, he is a liar; for he who does not love his brother whom he has seen, how can he love God whom he has not seen?

1 JOHN 4:20 NKJV

A greedy and grasping person
destroys community.
—PROVERBS 15:27 THE MESSAGE

Laugh with your friends when they're happy, share tears with them when they're down. Get along with each other; don't be stuck-up. Make friends with nobodies; don't be the great somebody.

ROMANS 12:15–16 THE MESSAGE

You, brethren, have been called to liberty; only do not use liberty as an opportunity for the flesh, but through love serve one another.

GALATIANS 5:13 NKJV

If you really fulfill the royal law according to the Scripture, "You shall love your neighbor as yourself," you do well; but if you show partiality, you commit sin, and are convicted by the law as transgressors.

JAMES 2:8–9 NKJV

Defend the poor and fatherless; do justice to the afflicted and needy. Deliver the poor and needy; free them from the hand of the wicked.

PSALM 82:3–4 NKJV

If one member suffers, all the members suffer with it; or if one member is honored, all the members rejoice with it.

1 CORINTHIANS 12:26 NKJV

Let all that you do be done with love.

1 CORINTHIANS 16:14 NKJV

Agree with each other. Love each other. Be deep-spirited friends.

PHILIPPIANS 2:2 THE MESSAGE

If you can help your neighbor now, don't say, "Come back tomorrow, and then I'll help you."

PROVERBS 3:28 NLT

If my heart is right with God, every human being is my neighbor.

—OSWALD CHAMBERS

Your neighbor is the man who is next to you at the moment, the man with whom any business has brought you into contact.

—GEORGE MACDONALD

Frustration

Pursuing Perfection

The LORD *will perfect that which concerns me; Your mercy, O* LORD, *endures forever; do not forsake the works of Your hands.*
—PSALM *138:8* NKJV

Here's a prescription for frustration: Try to do everything perfectly all the time. Oh, you may tell yourself that you are being "sensible" and not expecting too much. But it's so easy to get caught up in plans and create unrealistic expectations of who you are and what you should be. You need to relax and memorize this motto: Do your best and let God do the rest.

When you try too hard to be perfect and totally in control, you create frustration. Life is a gift, but it's a gift with grit. Some days are just not going to be perfect hair days. Sometimes you'll try to achieve a goal and fall short. Tempers flair, rooms get messy, bodies get sick, and clothes wrinkle. It's all part of life.

What is your definition of a perfect woman? a perfect relationship? a perfect career? a perfect marriage? a perfect child? Does your definition of *perfect* get in the way of enjoying life as it really is? Can you become more comfortable with seeing yourself as someone who is loved and forgiven by God? Can you appreciate the beauties of home, family, relationships, work, and worship as works in progress instead of lacking in polished perfection?

Instead of trying so hard to measure up to some impossible standard of perfection, perhaps perfection needs to be redefined. The next time you have a bad-hair day, make a decision that you're not going to let it frustrate you. Instead, concentrate your energy on other, more positive aspects of your life. Remember that the people who know and love you usually look past the bad hair to see the real you. They're looking at your heart, not your hair. Give yourself grace the next time you start worrying about the ways your clothes, home, career, personality, or love life don't measure up to some artificial standard in a magazine. That's an airbrushed fantasy, not earthy reality.

Relax and learn to love the imperfections. Recognize that God creates beauty out of imperfections. The knot in the grain of a fine wood, the wrinkles on an older face that has seen and accepted a long life, the weathered look of old leather that's soft as butter, the broken-in shoes that are so comfortable to wear, and the nubby texture of a hand-knit garment are all reminders that perfection is in the eye of the beholder. You're a person in process, and when you give yourself to the processes of God, you'll discover a new and more beautiful definition of grace and perfection.

I Will

Do my best and let God do the rest. _____ yes _____ no

Be thankful for life as it is rather than as I wish
it could be. _____ yes _____ no

Be thankful for the blessings in my life. _____ yes _____ no

Not judge a gift by the package it comes in. _____ yes _____ no

Be appreciative of the small things in life. _____ yes _____ no

Relax and be easier on myself and others. _____ yes _____ no

Redefine my definition of perfection to include
the beauties of imperfection. _____ yes _____ no

Things to Do

☐ Post a copy of 2 Corinthians 12:9 over your makeup mirror.

☐ Start a craft or art project that can teach you about the process of
creativity—and think about the ways you are in process in God's hands.

☐ Write in your journal about perfection: what you think it is, how you
have tried to achieve it, and ways you can redefine perfection to
embrace your life as it truly is.

☐ Watch a baby learning to walk.

☐ Go to an antique shop and think about the families that have used
these heirlooms and why that makes them beautiful, even with worn
spots and broken edges.

Things to Remember

Not that I have already attained all this, or have already been made perfect, but I press on to take hold of that for which Christ Jesus took hold of me.

PHILIPPIANS 3:12 NIV

God has chosen the foolish things of the world to put to shame the wise; and God has chosen the weak things of the world to put to shame the things which are mighty; and the base things of the world and the things which are despised God has chosen, and the things which are not, to bring to nothing the things that are, that no flesh should glory in His presence.

1 CORINTHIANS 1:27–29 NKJV

We have this treasure in earthen vessels, that the excellence of the power may be of God and not of us.

2 CORINTHIANS 4:7 NKJV

He said to me, "My grace is sufficient for you, for My strength is made perfect in weakness."

2 CORINTHIANS 12:9 NKJV

Let patience have its perfect work, that you may be perfect and complete, lacking nothing.

JAMES 1:4 NKJV

Perfection never exists apart from imperfection, just as good health cannot exist without our feeling effort, fatigue, hunger or thirst, heat or cold; yet none of these prevent the enjoyment of good health.

—HENRI DE TOURVILLE

Demand perfection of yourself and you'll seldom attain it. Fear of making a mistake is the single biggest cause of making one. Relax—pursue excellence, not perfection.

—BUD WINTER

Encouragement

A Warm Shoulder in a Cold World

Let us consider one another in order to stir up love and good works, not forsaking the assembling of ourselves together, as is the manner of some, but exhorting one another, and so much the more as you see the Day approaching.

—*HEBREWS 10:24–25* NKJV

Encouragement is a gift that we can offer others and ourselves. A listening ear, a warm shoulder to lean on, a helping hand, and an understanding heart offer support through the challenges and changes of life. When you make a conscious choice to be an encourager, you become God's helping hand of support, inspiring courage, hope, and confidence in the midst of a weary world.

When your best girlfriend tells you about her pet project, you respond with an enthusiastic "What a great idea! I know you'll make it happen." When the man in your life shares his hopes and dreams, you reinforce his self-worth and repel negative thoughts. You quietly say, "Yes, you can" instead of "Yes, but." You're not afraid to say something positive to others. These phrases are often a part of your conversation: "I love you because . . ." "I see in you . . ." "You're so good at . . ." "I like the way you . . ." "I know you will . . ."

Here are some tips for being a better encourager:

• Be specific and tell people in detail exactly what you like about them, what you have observed that can help them.

• Be honest and kind. No flattery allowed. You want to point out the positives, yet be someone who offers a dependable perspective, not a flattering lie.

• Be positive and confident. Express doubts with care and try to offer alternatives when you think someone is being unrealistic.

• Be spontaneous. Listen to what your heart says and be willing to speak it.

• Don't worry about how your encouragement is received. People are insecure and often don't know how to take praise. They often need time to revise the way they look at themselves. Just keep believing the best for them, even when they are afraid to believe it for themselves.

• Be consistent. Focus on the positive, make it a lifestyle. Make encouragement a habit.

• Offer suggestions, not advice. Honor each person's choices and believe in others' ability to navigate their own course. You may disagree with their decisions, but you have to respect their choices.

• Finally, be your own best encourager. Count your blessings. Be careful of the company you keep—don't spend too much time with negative people who tear one another down. Focus on the larger vision, knowing that God has called you to a unique work in this world. Give yourself time, space, and grace. Release your discouragement to God. Ask Him to help you find purpose in your pain and disappointments. Believe for the best.

I Will

Cultivate the art of encouraging others.   _yes_   _no_

Be honest, yet kind and helpful.   _yes_   _no_

Release my discouragement to God.   _yes_   _no_

Focus on the positive.   _yes_   _no_

Make encouragement a habit.   _yes_   _no_

Believe the best of others.   _yes_   _no_

Be willing to speak up and encourage others.   _yes_   _no_

Count my blessings.   _yes_   _no_

Things to Do

☐ Do a word study on encouragement.

☐ Call a friend and encourage her.

☐ Form an encouragers circle to meet on a regular basis.

☐ Offer to pray for someone else's needs.

☐ List specific ways someone is a blessing to you. Share the list with that person.

☐ Write a note of encouragement to five people.

☐ Give five people a loving hug today.

Things to Remember

Therefore let us pursue the things which make for peace and the things by which one may edify another.

ROMANS 14:9 NKJV

He answered, "Do not fear, for those who are with us are more than those who are with them."

2 KINGS 6:16 NKJV

They encouraged the followers and begged them to remain faithful.

ACTS 14:22 CEV

We treated each of you as a father treats his own children. We pleaded with you, encouraged you, and urged you to live your lives in a way that God would consider worthy.

1 THESSALONIANS 2:11–12 NLT

Let's see how inventive we can be in encouraging love and helping out.

HEBREWS 10:24 THE MESSAGE

Proclaim the message; be persistent whether the time is favorable or unfavorable; convince, rebuke, and encourage, with the utmost patience in teaching.

2 TIMOTHY 4:2 NRSV

Encouragement is oxygen to the soul.
—GEORGE M. ADAMS

Everybody can be great. Because anybody can serve. . . . You only need a heart full of grace. A soul generated by love.
—MARTIN LUTHER KING

Journeys

The Art of Pilgrimage

Our steps are made firm by the Lord, when he delights in our way.

—PSALM 37:23 NRSV

Life is a journey. You can choose to make this life a pilgrimage of faith and trust. You can proclaim, "I may not know where I'm going, but I know who's going with me." Like those who have traveled the pilgrim's path, you can walk with God every day.

You can look at life's journey in many ways. Think of the passages of life that all people go through. These personal journeys go not only across time and space, but also through epochs in your life. Think about the great adventure of childhood, when you became aware of yourself and then discovered the world beyond the family home. Remember adolescence, when the first signs of budding womanhood appeared, and you awkwardly began to reach out for adulthood. These are stages in life's journey and are journeys in and of themselves: the first time to live away from home, searching for a place to belong in the working world, finding compatible social circles, the commitment to a marriage, starting a family and watching your own children begin their own life journeys, letting go of aging parents as they move toward the great mystery beyond this life.

What do you need to take with you on a life journey? The Bible is an excellent map, offering eternal perspective on the territory you are passing through. The Spirit speaking to your heart is a compass that always points to the true north of God's love. A staff of faith to lean on and sturdy trust that God will guide you help keep you moving steadily forward. A grateful heart makes a cheery companion along the way, lightening loads and pointing out unexpected delights along the path. Friends and loved ones who share the journey make the road less lonely and light the way with love and encouragement.

God calls you out of the comfortable and familiar into new adventures. Just when you think you're settled in, something sets you off on a new pilgrimage. A crisis may make you reevaluate your life and decide on a new direction. A tragedy or loss can push you to create a life without someone or something you thought would always be there. Situations change, priorities shift, and suddenly you find yourself a wandering pilgrim once again, learning new lessons about trusting God.

You can also voluntarily seek out new adventures and begin journeys of faith. The great adventure of starting your own business can become an absorbing pilgrimage among business plans, suppliers, customers, and all the challenges inherent in being an entrepreneur. The choice to marry one man out of all the men in the world will change your life forever. Bringing a child into the world touches eternity and earth in a way that mere words can never describe. Making a move to another town, deciding to learn a new skill, giving yourself permission to pursue a dream, returning to school, taking a trip to a long dreamed-of destination—all of these are journeys that can be taken with a pilgrim heart.

As you travel along your pilgrim way, here are a few things to keep in mind:

A true pilgrim heart is a thankful heart. Whether it rains or the sun shines, an attitude of gratitude values the gifts that each day brings.

Plan to be flexible on a pilgrimage. Expect the unexpected. Rigid self protection and unrealistic expectations make things more difficult. Relax and go with the flow. You may have a good idea of your destination, but God often chooses to lead you by another path.

Instead of getting angry at detours and delays, be determined to learn the lessons that difficult times teach. See them as gifts that prepare you for the next stage of the journey.

Expect to be changed. Know that at the end of the journey you will be a different woman than the one who began the pilgrimage. God loves you as you are, but He loves you too much to let you stay where you are.

Place your trust in God. He will lead you safely through the detours, difficulties, and disasters that trouble you. His way is always safer than a known way. He always leads pilgrims safely to their destination.

Wait passionately for God, don't leave the path.

—Psalm 37:34 THE MESSAGE

I Will

Trust that God is with me every step along the way.   yes _____   no _____

Be open to new experiences and new ideas.   yes _____   no _____

Have a grateful heart.   yes _____   no _____

Be flexible.   yes _____   no _____

Look for rainbows when it rains.   yes _____   no _____

Learn the lessons difficulties can teach.   yes _____   no _____

Expect that I will change and grow as a person in
my journey through life.   yes _____   no _____

Things to Do

- [ ] Do a Bible study on someone who went on a journey, such as Abraham and Sarah, Joseph, Moses, Paul, Ruth and Naomi.

- [ ] Read John Bunyan's spiritual classic, A Pilgrim's Progress.

- [ ] Read a great adventure novel or a travel memoir.

- [ ] Go on a trip to a place you've never been to before.

- [ ] Take a long walk or drive in the country.

- [ ] In your journal, answer this question: If my life is a journey, where am I on that journey?

- [ ] Buy a guidebook and plan an imaginary journey to that destination.

Things to Remember

When I remember these things, I pour out my soul within me, for I used to go with the multitude; I went with them to the house of God, with the voice of joy and praise, with a multitude that kept a pilgrim feast.

PSALM 42:4 NKJV

These all died in faith, not having received the promises, but having seen them afar off were assured of them, embraced them, and confessed that they were strangers and pilgrims on earth.

HEBREWS 11:13 NKJV

Your statutes have been my songs in the house of my pilgrimage.
PSALM 119:54 NKJV

Your life is a journey you must travel with a deep consciousness of God. It cost God plenty to get you out of that dead-end, empty-headed life you grew up in.

1 PETER 1:17–18 THE MESSAGE

We walk by faith, not by sight.

2 CORINTHIANS 5:7 NKJV

Blessed are those whose strength is in you, who have set their hearts on pilgrimage.

PSALM 84:5 NIV

The LORD will command His lovingkindness in the daytime, and in the night His song shall be with me—a prayer to the God of my life.

PSALM 42:8 NKJV

The LORD had said to Abram: Get out of your country, from your family and from your father's house, to a land that I will show you.

GENESIS 12:1 NKJV

By faith Abraham obeyed when he was called to go out to the place which he would receive as an inheritance. And he went out, not knowing where he was going.

HEBREWS 11:8 NKJV

They desire a better, that is, a heavenly country. Therefore God is not ashamed to be called their God, for He has prepared a city for them.

HEBREWS 11:16 NKJV

We are the temple of the living God. As God said: "I will live in them and walk among them. I will be their God, and they will be my people."

2 CORINTHIANS 6:16 NLT

In the spiritual journey we travel through the night toward the day. We walk not in the bright sunshine of total certainty but through the darkness of ignorance, error, muddle, and uncertainty. We make progress in the journey as we grow in faith.

—CHRISTOPHER BRYANT

Every man has two journeys to make through life. There is the outer journey, with its various incidents and the milestones. . . . There is also an inner journey, a spiritual Odyssey, with a secret history of its own.

—WILLIAM RALPH INGE

Mistakes

Stop Kicking Yourself

Sin shall not have dominion over you, for you are not under law but under grace.

—ROMANS 6:14 NKJV

Mistakes happen. What counts is what you do with them. Instead of kicking yourself, learn from them. Let them be your teachers.

You get frustrated, especially when you make the same mistakes time and time again. So you get angry. You yell at yourself and call yourself names. Words like *failure* and *stupid* fall too easily from your lips. But mistakes are part of the learning process. When an artist makes a mistake, it often leads to an unexpected result—a more beautiful work of art. When God sees a "mistake," He understands and forgives. Even more, He transforms the mistake and its consequences into a way to help you grow and develop. A mistake is a lesson, an opportunity to learn.

Watch a child learn to walk. She doesn't fall and then decide she's never going to get up again. No, something deep inside impels her to keep trying. Up again on unsteady legs, ready to try once more. No matter how many times she falls, she picks herself up and goes at it again. She doesn't cripple herself with an inner dialogue that says she's a failure for falling. She doesn't concentrate on the fall, but on the goal of getting up and walking. Deep down inside, she knows she can do it. She was born to walk and she knows it. And when the little girl triumphantly takes her first steps, all the falls are forgotten in the glee of accomplishment. "Mommy's good girl is walking. Yes!"

So it is with you. If you keep making the same mistakes over and over again, it is a signal that you have a lesson to learn. Perhaps you need to try a different way of doing things. Perhaps there is some skill that you need to develop or some confidence that you have to build. Just as an artist doesn't immediately produce a polished masterpiece, so you may have some more things to work through. Perhaps like the child learning to walk, the falls you take are just part of the natural process of reaching your goal. We are all people in process.

What about the mistakes and failures that hurt others? Trust God and His mercy. Ask His forgiveness and, if appropriate, ask the forgiveness of those who have been hurt by your actions. He forgives you and will help you deal with the consequences of your mistakes. Learn from your mistakes and move on. Mistakes are your teachers, if you will allow them to teach you.

I Will

Trust God and do my best.   yes ___ no ___

Believe that God forgives me.   yes ___ no ___

Learn from my mistakes.   yes ___ no ___

Forgive others.   yes ___ no ___

Forgive myself.   yes ___ no ___

Be flexible.   yes ___ no ___

Be willing to be a beginner.   yes ___ no ___

Be willing to try a different way.   yes ___ no ___

Things to Do

☐ Memorize a Bible verse about God's forgiveness, such as Isaiah 1:18.

☐ Do a word study on forgiveness.

☐ Watch a child learning to walk.

☐ Make a collage of twenty images that remind you of freedom and forgiveness.

☐ Go to someone who has been hurt by one of your mistakes and ask forgiveness for your part in the problem.

☐ Start an art or craft project and deliberately make a mistake. Now see what beautiful thing you can create from that "mistake."

Things to Remember

Is it not clear to you that to go back to that old rule-keeping, peer-pleasing religion would be an abandonment of everything personal and free in my relationship with God? I refuse to do that, to repudiate God's grace. If a living relationship with God could come by rule keeping, then Christ died unnecessarily.

GALATIANS 2:21 THE MESSAGE

I will be merciful to their unrighteousness, and their sins and their lawless deeds I will remember no more.

HEBREWS 8:12 NKJV

If anyone is in Christ, he is a new creation; old things have passed away; behold, all things have become new.

2 CORINTHIANS 5:17 NKJV

If our heart condemns us, God is greater than our heart, and knows all things.

1 JOHN 3:20 NKJV

Whoever catches a glimpse of the revealed counsel of God—the free life!—even out of the corner of his eye, and sticks with it, is no distracted scatterbrain but a man or woman of action. That person will find delight and affirmation in the action.

JAMES 1:25 THE MESSAGE

A man should never be ashamed to own he has been in the wrong, which is but saying, in other words, that he is wiser today than he was yesterday.

—JONATHAN SWIFT

The man who makes no mistakes does not usually make anything.

—EDWARD JOHN PHELPS

Sickness

Let the Fever Run Its Course

The LORD will strengthen him on his bed of illness; You will sustain him on his sickbed.

—*PSALM 41:3* NKJV

You've been going, going, going for days now. You've been running on adrenaline, trying to squeeze too much into your schedule. Suddenly you get a headache. Then a sniffle. Then a full-blown sneeze. Before you know it, you've collapsed into bed with an achy tired body. There are still a million things you have to do, but it doesn't matter. You are sick and your body has called a time out.

Sickness is a sign that something needs attention. Your body is signaling that it's time to rest and take care of yourself. If you ignore the symptoms, you could develop more lasting problems and end up with a serious long-term illness. Respect the natural rhythm of being sick and getting well. Let the fever run its course and allow your body to heal itself.

Being sick is an opportunity to learn a few lessons. You learn the lesson that you are not indispensable. The world does not stop because you are ill. It goes on without you. Yet when you are well again, you usually discover that the world has room for you to return and become part of the great wheel of life. All the plans you made were good and important, but not so important that you can't take time to heal.

This enforced time out offers an opportunity to reevaluate your life. It reminds you that you need to take care of yourself. It is also an opportunity to hear from God in a fresh way, learning that ultimately God is in charge of your life. Many women have discovered that a serious illness becomes the catalyst for creating a more satisfying life. When you come close to death, your priorities change. Those who are fortunate enough to return to full health create a new "normal" that takes into account the limitations of their bodies and the desires of their hearts.

Keep in mind that it takes time to get well. Nature works her healing magic only when we allow her time and rest to do it. The body is not a machine to ignore and abuse but is a friend who tells you something is out of balance and needs to be changed.

As you recover and begin to get well, keep in mind that reentry can be slow. Take it easy at first. Don't overdo. And recognize that you may need to learn to pace yourself in a new way once the fever has run its course and you're back on your feet again.

I Will

Choose to trust God in times of illness.   *yes*   *no*

Listen to what the Spirit of the Lord has to say
to me when I am sick.   *yes*   *no*

Use illness as a time to reconsider my priorities.   *yes*   *no*

Rest in God's love.   *yes*   *no*

Slow down and let nature's healing
processes happen.   *yes*   *no*

Take better care of myself.   *yes*   *no*

Honor my body in sickness and in health.   *yes*   *no*

Things to Do

☐ Read about the healing miracles in the Gospels.

☐ When you are feeling stressed out and on the edge of getting sick, take
a day to rest and renew (before illness can develop!).

☐ Make sure your medicine cabinet is stocked.

☐ Make a special treat basket for times of convalescence: magazines,
books, bedtime treats, puzzles, and special soaps.

☐ Take a treat basket to a sick friend.

☐ Go to bed an hour early tonight and get some needed rest.

☐ Write about your priorities in your journal—especially if your schedule
is running you ragged.

Things to Remember

Before I was afflicted I went astray, but now I keep Your word, You are good, and do good; teach me Your statutes.

PSALM 119:67–68 NKJV

Heal me, O LORD, and I shall be healed; save me, and I shall be saved, for You are my praise.

JEREMIAH 17:14 NKJV

The LORD said, "Behold, I will bring it health and healing; I will heal them and reveal to them the abundance of peace and truth."

JEREMIAH 33:6 NKJV

Jesus went about all the cities and villages, teaching in their synagogues, preaching the gospel of the kingdom, and healing every sickness and every disease among the people.

MATTHEW 9:35 NKJV

Jesus turned him about, and when he saw her, he said, Daughter, be of good comfort, thy faith hath made thee whole. And the woman was made whole from that hour.

MATTHEW 9:22 KJV

He sent His word and healed them, and delivered them from their destructions.

PSALM 107:20 NKJV

In a time of sickness the soul collects itself anew.

—LATIN PROVERB

If you should get ill, through circumstances beyond your control, bear it patiently and wait patiently upon God's mercy. That is all you need to do. It is true to say that patience in sickness and other forms of trouble pleases God much more than any splendid devotion you might show in health.

—THE CLOUD OF UNKNOWING

Goals

Creating the Future

~~~~~~

Many are the plans in a man's heart, but it is the LORD's *purpose that prevails.*

—PROVERBS 19:21 NIV

You're standing at a crossroads. You may have success in your past, but now it's time for growth and change. You may have limitations and failures in the past, but now it's time to create a new future with wider horizons. It's time to set some new goals.

Here are some key questions to ask yourself as you think about your goals:

What is it that I really want to achieve? Don't limit yourself to what you think you can do or ask how it will be done. Dare to dream beyond self-imposed limitations. Seek your true heart's desire first. Then decide how to reach that goal later.

What do I need to stop doing so that I can start doing what I want to do? Learn to say no to what you don't want. Give yourself permission to say yes to what you do want.

What commitment am I willing to make? Change always takes more time than you think it will. If you start asking how long it will take, you're asking the wrong question. It is easy to underestimate what it takes to reach your goal. Choose a goal that is worthwhile and vitally important to you, and you'll be able to make a full commitment to that goal. How long does it take to raise a child? Change a culture? Create a new direction?

What price are you willing to pay? How much do you value this goal? The price of change is effort, will, courage, and perseverance. Are you willing to risk failure and getting hurt if it doesn't work out? If the goal is worthy, it will be worth the risk. The very act of pursuing a worthwhile goal can change you for the better, whether or not you catch the star you're reaching for.

What is my contribution? Look at how you contribute to the problem. Then ask how you can contribute to the solution. This is not about what others are doing, but about who you are and what you choose to become.

What do I want to create? Who do I want to create it with? Visualize the end result of reaching your goal. Is this a reality you would be happy to live in? Who do you want to share this reality?

Pray and ask God to be with you in the process of dreaming, planning, and working toward your goals. He wants to be your partner, helping you and guiding you throughout the entire process.

I Will

Pray and trust that God is with me as I set goals and
work toward them.   *yes*   *no*

Seek my heart's deepest desires.   *yes*   *no*

Create a positive future.   *yes*   *no*

Make commitments and stick with them.   *yes*   *no*

Be willing to make changes when necessary.   *yes*   *no*

Look for ways I can contribute to the solution instead
of the problem.   *yes*   *no*

Face the future with courage and hope.   *yes*   *no*

Things to Do

☐ Pray about your goals and ask God to guide you as you seek a better
future.

☐ Set a simple goal for this week and achieve that goal.

☐ Make a list of goals you would like to achieve in the next week; month;
year; five years; ten years.

☐ Visualize a cherished goal. Imagine what it would feel like to achieve
that goal and write about it in your journal.

☐ Take a class or buy a book on life planning.

☐ Share goals with a group of friends and encourage each other as you
take steps toward achieving those goals.

Things to Remember

I press toward the goal for the prize of the upward call of God in Christ Jesus.

PHILIPPIANS 3:14 NKJV

Jesus said to him, "If you can believe, all things are possible to him who believes."

MARK 9:23 NKJV

Figure out what will please Christ, and then do it.

EPHESIANS 5:10 THE MESSAGE

These are the ones sown on good ground, those who hear the word, accept it, and bear fruit; some thirtyfold, some sixty, and some a hundred.

MARK 4:20 NKJV

Be diligent to present yourself approved to God, a worker who does not need to be ashamed, rightly dividing the word of truth.

2 TIMOTHY 2:15 NKJV

Do not become sluggish, but imitate those who through faith and patience inherit the promises.

HEBREWS 6:12 NKJV

Your imagination is your preview of life's coming attractions.

—ALBERT EINSTEIN

Those who believe they can and those who believe they can't are both right.

—ANONYMOUS

Entrepeneurs

Owning Your Own Business

She perceives that her merchandise is good, and her lamp does not go out by night.

—*Proverbs 31:18* NKJV

Is your work challenging, stimulating, and a reflection of who you are? Or do you feel like you're in a dead-end job, always watching the clock and living for the weekends? If you want to create a work life that expresses who you are and reflects your highest values, consider owning your own business.

Over a million businesses start in the U.S. every year. Women are starting new businesses twice as fast as men. More and more women are choosing to start businesses—from one-person home businesses to multimillion-dollar corporations. Women are more likely to start a business because they have hit the glass ceiling in their climb up the corporate ladder, want to spend more time with their children, need more flexibility in their schedules, or have a passion they want to pursue.

Women-run businesses come in all sizes and shapes. One

woman might open a local flower shop, another might create a dried-flower crafts business, and another build a national flower-delivery empire. From consultants to creative artists, from stockbrokers to secretarial services, women are creating businesses that suit their lifestyles and offer them the opportunity to pursue a passionate interest and make a profit at the same time.

What does it take to make a success of your own business?

• Persistence: You need to be able to push ahead, having what it takes to plug away a little at a time, day after day, until a job is done.

• Ability to face the facts: You need to be able to constantly reevaluate changing situations, learning, adjusting, and changing your behavior when your way of doing things no longer works.

• Ability to minimize risks: While being open to new ideas, you also need to make fall-back plans and seek alternative solutions, constantly and methodically looking for ways to reduce risk and get the most out of resources.

• Willingness to be a hands-on learner: Participating in the total process, you learn by doing. Every business is a learning laboratory, and every business owner needs to understand all aspects of the business.

• Market-focused perspective: You need to be able to find and focus on your appropriate market niche. Know what you want to sell, whom you want to sell to, what need your product or service fills, and how you can reach those who want to buy.

• Cooperative attitude: There is more power in cooperation than in cutthroat competition. Even with a one-person business working out of your home, you'll have to work with clients, customers, suppliers, and people who provide services to your business, such as accountants and consultants. You live in a community, and your business functions in the matrix of that community.

• Confidence: You need to be wise enough to ask questions and confident enough to make your own decisions and stick with them.

• Faith: You have to have faith in yourself and believe that it's possible to succeed. There will be many challenges and obstacles to overcome as you plan and build your business. Your faith in God and reliance on His help and guidance will also give you strength to pursue your dreams and reach your goals.

These qualities will stand you in good stead whether you decide to start your own business or to continue building your career where you are already employed. Stay-at-home mothers, women who work as volunteers in community or church organizations, or those who for one reason or another choose not to work in a traditional job can also develop these entrepreneurial qualities in their daily accomplishments. Employees can bring an entrepreneurial spirit to their own jobs, becoming intrapreneurs who create greater value for the companies where they work.

For women who want to live their faith out in meaningful ways, the workplace offers a wonderful opportunity to grow as a person and live out your faith in practical ways. Being a business owner can be satisfying, but it's not for everyone. Women who have successfully struck out on their own have discovered a satisfying lifestyle—and have also discovered that starting a business takes faith as much as hard work. God is interested in being your partner in all your endeavors. Let Him be your unseen business partner, a fellow entrepreneur who supports you on the great adventure of creating a successful business career.

I Will

Trust in God as my career counselor and
business partner.   *yes*   *no*

Be willing to learn by doing.   *yes*   *no*

Work smart as well as working hard.   *yes*   *no*

Be honest about my strengths and my weaknesses. *yes*   *no*

Have faith in my ability to succeed.   *yes*   *no*

Be persistent.   *yes*   *no*

Have a professional attitude.   *yes*   *no*

Focus on an appropriate market niche.   *yes*   *no*

Things to Do

☐ Write in your journal about where you would like to be in a year and
what you would like to be doing.

☐ Take a business class from your local small-business resource center or
community college.

☐ Learn about basic bookkeeping and business recordkeeping.

☐ Go to a job fair or a business convention and learn more about the
business/career you are interested in.

☐ Apprentice yourself to someone who has experience in the field you
want to enter or work in your field (for example, take an entry-level job
in a shop if you want to learn about the craft business) before you
commit to starting your own business.

Things to Remember

You shall remember the LORD your God, for it is He who gives you power to get wealth, that He may establish His covenant which He swore to your fathers, as it is this day.

DEUTERONOMY 8:18 NKJV

The LORD will command the blessing on you in your storehouses and in all to which you put your hand, and He will bless you in the land which the LORD your God is giving you.

DEUTERONOMY 28:8 NKJV

Whatever your task, put yourselves into it, as done for the Lord and not for your masters.
—COLOSSIANS 3:23 NRSV

Well-done work has its own reward.

PROVERBS 12:14 THE MESSAGE

Whatsoever thy hand findeth to do, do it with thy might.

ECCLESIASTES 9:10 KJV

As long as I'm alive in this body, there is good work for me to do.

PHILIPPIANS 1:22 THE MESSAGE

Don't hold back. Throw yourselves into the work of the Master, confident that nothing you do for him is a waste of time or effort.

1 CORINTHIANS 15:58 THE MESSAGE

Observe people who are good at their work—skilled workers are always in demand and admired.

PROVERBS 22:29 THE MESSAGE

When you eat the labor of your hands, you shall be happy, and it shall be well with you.

PSALM 128:2 NKJV

You don't need a lot of equipment. You are the equipment, and all you need to keep that going is three meals a day. Travel light.

MATTHEW 10:10 THE MESSAGE

Honest balances and scales are the LORD's; all the weights in the bag are his work.

PROVERBS 16:11 NRSV

All goes well for those who are generous, who lend freely and conduct their business fairly.

PSALM 112:5 NLT

Work is not primarily a thing one does to live, but the thing one lives to do.

—DOROTHY SAYERS

Whatever you can do or dream you can, begin it. Boldness has genius, power, and magic in it.

—GOETHE

Words

Watch Your Mouth

A soft answer turns away wrath, but a harsh word stirs up anger.

—*Proverbs 15:1* NKJV

Be careful how you use words. Words have great power. They can make or break relationships, make life easier, or make life drearier. The Bible says to "speak the truth in love," but sometimes it's hard to find a balance between being honest and loving. You need God's wisdom to help you keep a watch over what you say and how you say it—and why you say it.

It's easy to criticize others—and yourself. You live in a society of armchair critics. Thumbs up, thumbs down. Grading on the curve. Reviews of books, TV shows, movies, and the arts. Radio talk shows critiquing everything from government to personalities. It's easy to become a critic when so many opinions are expressed so frequently and frankly. But if you want to nurture and develop your relationships, you need to keep criticism at a minimum and emphasize encouraging and kind words instead. Think of the parody of "Home on the Range": "Home, home on the range, where the deer and the antelope play; where seldom is heard a discouraging word, for what can an antelope say?" Sometimes when you are thinking critical thoughts it is wisest to be like an antelope and say nothing.

You need to be honest, but wisdom balances honesty with kindness and sensitivity. The truth must be told in love, not judgment or condemnation. Difficult truths need to be well presented and well timed. Even when someone asks for a critique, you need to weigh your words, sensing what they are ready to hear and what needs to be held back for a later time. Respect the process of personal growth, realizing that there is a time for words and a time for silence.

Don't be shy about encouraging or complimenting someone, either. Because society sends so many critical messages, people are hungry to hear the loving encouragement that tells them that they are unique and wonderful human beings. Be generous with your praise. Become aware of the special gifts each person brings into your life and say in specific ways how you have been blessed or inspired by him or her.

Watch your comments about situations. Are you consistently negative? Or do you look for and speak about the positive? Monitor your speech and deliberately choose positive words. A positive attitude creates more positives. Ask God to help you keep a guard on your tongue. He will teach you how to speak words of honest wisdom and loving-kindness.

I Will

Ask for God's wisdom in all I say.   _yes_   _no_

Compliment others frequently.   _yes_   _no_

Be honest in what I say to others.   _yes_   _no_

Be kind and compassionate.   _yes_   _no_

Speak the truth in love.   _yes_   _no_

Be generous with praise.   _yes_   _no_

Encourage others (and myself) instead of
criticizing and tearing them down.   _yes_   _no_

Things to Do

☐ Do a Bible study on words and the power of the tongue.

☐ Write an encouraging note to a friend who is struggling.

☐ Get together with friends and encourage one another.

☐ Make a list of twenty things you like about yourself. Be specific.

☐ Give someone an honest compliment today.

☐ Just for one day, replace every negative comment you would make with a positive comment.

☐ Write in your journal your thoughts on the difference between flattery and praise.

Things to Remember

Even a fool is thought wise if he keeps silent, and discerning if he holds his tongue.

PROVERBS 17:28 NIV

The words of a man's mouth are deep waters; the wellspring of wisdom is a flowing brook.

PROVERBS 18:4 NKJV

He who covers a transgression seeks love, but he who repeats a matter separates friends.

PROVERBS 17:9 NKJV

Above all things have fervent love for one another, for "love will cover a multitude of sins."

1 PETER 4:8 NKJV

Don't pick on people, jump on their failures, criticize their faults—unless, of course, you want the same treatment. Don't condemn those who are down; that hardness can boomerang. Be easy on people; you'll find life a lot easier.

LUKE 6:37 THE MESSAGE

She opens her mouth with wisdom, and on her tongue is the law of kindness.

PSALM 31:26 NKJV

Words which do not give the light of Christ increase the darkness.

—MOTHER TERESA

Be kind. Remember that everyone you meet is fighting a hard battle.

—HARRY THOMPSON

Patience

Waiting on God

Hope deferred makes the heart sick, but when the desire comes, it is a tree of life.

—PROVERBS 13:12 NKJV

How many times have you found yourself asking impatiently, "How long is this going to take?" Yet God's timing is different from yours, and you may often find yourself in need of patience. You may think that you are too busy to wait, to allow things to grow naturally. You force solutions, often creating more problems than you solve. But God works in His own time and in His own way. He teaches you the value of patience. In the larger perspective of life, eternal lessons teach you that patience is required for the things that are really important.

It takes time to raise a child, nurture a relationship, grow a career, and create a community. The Scriptures use the image of a farmer patiently waiting for seed, soil, sun, and rain to do its work. The field must be plowed, the seed sown, the land fertilized and watered, the soil weeded, and the crop tended before it comes to full fruition. So it is with you.

When you cultivate patience, you are growing the fruit

of the Spirit in your life. Patience is not passiveness, but a proactive faith that is willing to trust God in the midst of difficulties and delays.

How do you cultivate patience during times of waiting? Here are some ideas:

• Take it one day at a time. Instead of trying to second-guess the future, look at what you have right now. What can be accomplished today? Concentrate only on what you are able to do today and put tomorrow in God's hands.

• Do what you can and let go of trying to control the outcome. All you can do is do your best and leave the rest up to God. In most of the important things in life, we are dependent on God's grace.

• Write in your journal. Write about your feelings of impatience. Imagine the fulfillment of your desires and write that down. Remember times when your patience was rewarded. A journal is a safe place to vent, to dream, and to track answers to prayer requests.

• Meditate on Scripture. The Bible offers a timeless way of looking at life and we absorb that larger perspective when we feed our spirits with the Word.

• Pray. Bring your worries, frustrations, and anxiety to God. Tell Him how you honestly feel and ask His help in being patient. Speak words of faith affirming that you trust Him to bring things to full fruition in His perfect timing.

I Will

Cultivate a patient attitude.	yes	no
Trust God with my future.	yes	no
Bring my worries and anxieties to God in prayer.	yes	no
Take life one day at a time.	yes	no
Avoid second-guessing the future.	yes	no
Affirm my trust in God with words of faith.	yes	no
Depend on God's grace and divine timing.	yes	no
Do my best and leave the rest up to God.	yes	no

Things to Do

☐ Write in your journal about a time when God rewarded your patient work and waiting.

☐ Write in your journal about a time when you tried to make something happen and it fell apart.

☐ Meditate on a favorite verse about patience (perhaps James 5:7–8). Write it on a 3 x 5 card and post it on your bathroom mirror.

☐ The next time you find yourself getting impatient, take a time out.

☐ Go over your personal calendar and see if you are trying to do too much in too little time. Eliminate one unnecessary activity.

☐ Plant a seed and wait for it to sprout.

Things to Remember

My friends, be patient until the Lord
returns. Think of farmers who wait
patiently for the spring and summer
rains to make their valuable crops grow.
Be patient like those farmers and don't
give up.

JAMES 5:7–8 CEV

Be glad for all God is planning for you.
Be patient in trouble, and always be
prayerful.

ROMANS 12:12 NLT

Jesus said, "In your patience possess
your souls."

LUKE 21:19 NKJV

After he had patiently endured, he
obtained the promise.

HEBREWS 6:15 NKJV

Be still before the LORD, and wait
patiently for him, do not fret over those
who prosper in their way, over those
who carry out evil devices.

PSALM 37:7 NRSV

I waited patiently for the LORD; and He
inclined to me, and heard my cry.

PSALM 40:1 NKJV

*Teach us, O Lord,
the disciplines of
patience, for to wait
is often harder than
to work.*

—PETER MARSHALL

*On every level of life
from housework to
the heights of prayer,
in all judgement and
all efforts to get
things done, hurry
and impatience are
the sure marks of an
amateur.*

—EVELYN UNDERHILL

Mystery

Through a Glass Darkly

Now we see through a glass, darkly; but then, face to face: now I know in part; but then I shall know even as also I am known.
—1 CORINTHIANS 13:12 KJV

One of the most wonderful discoveries about the Christian life is that there is always more to discover. You have the privilege of knowing God, but you also find that the more you learn, the more you realize there is yet to understand. In all the joys and sorrows of life, God is with you. Yet at the same time, this known and loved heavenly Friend is also a great mystery, beyond all human understanding.

Sometimes you may want to put God in a box. Perhaps you like to have your answers pat, your explanations neat and tidy. When life gets messy and complicated, you want to have a God you can pull out of your back pocket. You want to order Him to fix things the way you want them to be. But God does not obey your commands. You can't just pop something in a cosmic vending machine and get canned answers and bottled solutions. People are finite and God is infinite and almighty. He will do what He pleases.

God has made Himself known. You know Him through nature and see Him reflected in your own human nature. We know Him because He has spoken to us in the Scriptures. And as a Christian, you have come to know Him through Jesus Christ, who you believe is fully God and yet also fully human, God coming to dwell with humankind in unimaginable ways in time and space. Yet you only touch the hem of His garment, even in these wonderful ways of knowing Him. To try to comprehend the vastness of the mystery of God is like trying to contain the ocean in a teacup.

All through history believers have struggled with the mystery of God and how He works in the world and in your heart. Read church history for an education on how each era grappled with the mystery of the incarnation, life, death, and resurrection of Christ—and how that made a difference for each believer in the midst of the culture he inhabited. It is written in Isaiah, "My thoughts are not your thoughts, my ways are not your ways." Read about the prophets and their difficulties as they tried to shake Israel out of a religious rut. Meditate on the ways Paul was transformed by his encounter with Christ on the road to Damascus. Read the stories of the early church, which thrived in the face of persecution. What a mystery—that people would come to the Christian faith because they saw the way Christians died in the Roman arena. God may have shut the lions' mouths when the prophet Daniel was thrown in the lions' den, but the blood of martyrs was on the sand when the first Christians faced the roaring beasts. Ponder the life of Abraham, who was told by God to look up at the stars and believe in a great nation; who left his homeland for an unseen promise from a mysterious God.

Like grass growing between the cracks of cement, even the most literal-minded person can be confronted with the mystery of God's transforming power. Your own life, however mundane as it might seem on the surface, is full of mystery. Why were you born to one particular family and no other? How did you meet the people who would change the course of your life? Why do some things resonate so deeply in your heart? What makes the dogwood outside your door open its blossoms in the spring? How to the birds know when to fly south for the winter? Why does your heart lift and sing at the sight of a round full moon? Why do you love one dear person so deeply and irrevocably?

The greatest mystery is the love of God. The Scriptures proclaim it, but you also experience it in the unexpected mercies of life. The accident you just missed by minutes. The miracle of birth. The wonder of one human being loving another.

Like Mary, ponder the mysteries of life in your heart. Be practical, yes. Make your lists of things to do and check them off one by one. Make logical choices and live a down-to-earth life. But also make room for moments to worship God in the beauty of holiness and to honor the mysteries of the human heart.

This is a great mystery, but it is an illustration of the way Christ and the church are one.

—Ephesians 5:32 NLT

I Will

Worship God in the beauty of mystery and holiness. _yes_ _no_

Let my heart sing with wonder. _yes_ _no_

Believe in the things I do not see. _yes_ _no_

Trust God when I do not understand. _yes_ _no_

Look for reminders of God's love in everyday things. _yes_ _no_

Embrace the mysteries of the human heart. _yes_ _no_

Make room for God to surprise me. _yes_ _no_

Things to Do

☐ Attend a worship service and meditate on God's greatness and mystery.

☐ Read a book on church history and learn how the church has grown and changed through the centuries (perhaps Eerdman's Handbook to the History of Christianity, Jesus Through the Centuries by Jaroslav Pelikan, or Christianity: A Global History by David Chidester).

☐ Read Psalm 19 aloud.

☐ Grow narcissi or other fragrant bulbs on a winter windowsill.

☐ Memorize all the verses of one of the great hymns of the church (for example, "O Sacred Head Now Wounded," "Amazing Grace," "O the Deep, Deep Love of Jesus," "Great Is Thy Faithfulness," or "A Mighty Fortress Is Our God").

Things to Remember

He has made everything beautiful in its time. He has also set eternity in the hearts of men; yet they cannot fathom what God has done from beginning to end.

ECCLESIASTES 3:1 NIV

Be assured that from the first day we heard of you, we haven't stopped praying for you, asking God to give you wise minds and spirits attuned to his will, and so acquire a thorough understanding of the ways in which God works.

COLOSSIANS 1:9 THE MESSAGE

Where were you when I laid the foundations of the earth? Tell Me, if you have understanding.

—JOB 38:4 NKJV

He reveals deep and hidden things; he knows what lies in darkness, and light dwells with him.

DANIEL 2:22 NIV

You asked, "Who is this who hides counsel without knowledge?" Therefore I have uttered what I did not understand, things too wonderful for me, which I did not know.

JOB 42:3 NKJV

Can you fathom the mysteries of God? Can you probe the limits of the Almighty?

JOB 11:7 NIV

Great is our Lord, and mighty in power;
His understanding is infinite.

PSALM 147:5 NKJV

I still have many things to say to you,
but you cannot bear them now.

JOHN 16:12 NKJV

Beyond all question, the mystery of
godliness is great: He appeared in a
body, was vindicated by the Spirit, was
seen by angels, was preached among the
nations, was believed on in the world,
was taken up in glory.

1 TIMOTHY 3:16 NIV

Oh, the depth of the riches both of the
wisdom and knowledge of God! How
unsearchable are His judgments and His
ways past finding out!

ROMANS 11:33 NKJV

God gave Solomon wisdom and
exceedingly great understanding.

1 KINGS 4:29 NKJV

Cry out for insight and understanding.

PROVERBS 2:3 NLT

True wisdom and power are with God;
counsel and understanding are his.

JOB 12:13 NLT

If you think you understand, it isn't God.

—SAINT AUGUSTINE

A religion without mystery must be a religion without God.

—JEREMY TAYLOR

Other Books in the Checklist for Life Series

Checklist for Life
ISBN 0-7852-6455-8

Checklist for Life for Men
ISBN 0-7852-6463-9

Checklist for Life for Teens
ISBN 0-7852-6461-2